LIVING IN THE FIRE

Pamela Flynt Knight

ARCHWAY
PUBLISHING

Archway Publishing books may be ordered through booksellers or by contacting:

Archway Publishing
1663 Liberty Drive
Bloomington, IN 47403
www.archwaypublishing.com
844-669-3957

ISBN: 978-1-6657-6386-8 (sc)
ISBN: 978-1-6657-6387-5 (e)

Library of Congress Control Number: 2024918482

Print information available on the last page.

Archway Publishing rev. date: 11/26/2024

BURNING UP OR BURNING UP SIN

This assessment will help you learn the difference. You want to make a difference in other people's lives but first you need to know where you stand.

➤ Navigate your life and trials
➤ Face your sins
➤ Listen to the Holy Spirit
➤ Search for answers to where God wants you
➤ See how you can affect other's lives

God speaks of fire throughout scripture. Walk through this personal enrichment with friends to learn how you are *Living in the Fire* on a daily basis.

DEDICATION

"being confident of this very thing, that he who be-
gan a good work in you will perfect it until the day
of Jesus Christ" (Philippians 1:6)

I want to dedicate this book to my Lord and Savior, Jesus Christ. He
never gave up on me getting this finished from the time he placed the
idea in my heart, through all the years it took to publish the first and
second editions.

Now with this personal enrichment, I pray that God will be glori-
fied, and many will learn how to follow His word closely.

THANKS

I want to thank Robert Shehane and Fred Johnson for their editing and
for their review of the theological ideals set forth in this publication.

A sincere thank you goes out to all those who have patiently waited
for the original work to be transformed into this second edition. May it
be a blessed addition to your study.

A thank you goes out to my son, Stephen Knight for his work on
the book cover design.

ACKNOWLEDGMENTS

I have used the American Standard Version of the Bible in this book.
Make note that there are over 500 acknowledgments of the word "fire"
in that version. I have used very few of these but I hope it will be a great
help to you in your life.

CONTENTS

||||||||||||||||||||||||||||||||||||||||||||||||||||||||||||||||||||||||||||||||||||||||||||||||||||||||||||||

Introducing The Beginning

This book has been a long time in the making. I was much younger when I started it. My confidence and enthusiasm waivered and the writing sat dormant for longer than I like to admit. But God used that time to refine me and to refine my faith. What could have turned out to be a very poor spotted memoire, has turned into a book that I believe can be helpful.

If it is helpful to only me, as I re-read and do re-writes, it has been helpful. I sometimes sit back astonished at a sentence or paragraph and think "Did I write that?" or "I needed that right now." So, I must admit that there is much more inspiration involved in this writing than my personal wisdom. I have shared personal experiences because I hope they will paint a picture for you and ignite your own remembrances.

I know that God is still working in my life and that His refining fire will always be present. I would hope that I pay closer attention today to what He tells me and obey His word quickly. The truth is I am still very fallible and often slow to learn or remember lessons from the past. I am glad that God is gracious and forgiving. How quickly we forget our lessons and God's great faithfulness!

I hope you will sit back and enjoy the nuggets from God that I have to share with you. I think some will speak to your heart and others you have experienced already and will just nod in agreement. Some may apply to you now and others will not mean anything until possibly a later date. And then there will be things you disagree with me about. (Help me now Jesus because my stubborn perfectionism does not want to admit to anything being wrong!) Maybe you will experience all the above.

I know when God deals with us, we sometimes get upset and begin to dig in and say we will have nothing to do with that kind of change. So, if at some point you dig in your heals, or throw this book across the room, please do not stop reading. When you persist, you will harvest more faith and understanding than you have currently. I have no doubt that God has something in here for you.

God is always changing us; refining us; so that we can be a beautiful reflection of Christ. You are His creation, and He wants the best for you. Becoming the best we can be, means we will have to experience change and difficult circumstances. Learn to rejoice through trials of life because you are *Living in the Fire* of God's perfection.

LIVING IN THE FIRE

Living in the Fire is not about instant miracles but living miracles. It is how God manifests through circumstances in our lives to give us the strength, knowledge, and understanding we will need much further down the road.

I have heard miracles defined as natural things that God reduces to our understanding. The universe is written in large letters, but miracles are written in small letters for us to see. I image an ant or flea crawling across the page of a book. All the ant can see is the black spot or white space it is on. The ant is unable to see the letters or words that make up the pages of the book; it is unable to see the whole story. The same is true of our lives. Each page is a new phase in our life.

By learning who we are through the eyes of God, the drag of insecurity is severed, our confidence is elevated, and our joy returns. In the book of Nehemiah, we are told that our strength comes from experiencing the joy of the Lord. In accepting this, we find our self-awareness and confidence in the Lord, not in what others think or society tells us.

In *Living the Fire*, we are going to examine the concept of fire, how it unfolds in scripture and how it applies to our lives. As you covenant with God, see how the refining fire of the Holy Spirit consecrates, guides, protects, reveals, tests, and consumes your own life – **all** for the glory of God.

As you read, be sure to search with your heart. Look within your heart. As you walk through life and live in the fire, seek God's heart.

See the joy and peace you can experience by resting in God's provision and trusting in His word through the trials of your life.

We are God's zeal, manifested for men to see, and fulfilled through love. Knowing that our source of strength, knowledge, understanding and confidence is in God makes it easier for us to understand how to be strong in the Lord and in the power of His might.[1] It is by seeking His face and accepting His joy.

This book is for all the people who are hurting, for all those who know God but do not know where He is right now in their lives. It is for all those who do not know God but need to know where He is right now. This book is for me, and it is for you. If you have not been in a place where you are questioning your life, you someday will be. I hope I can encourage you to hang in there no matter what. You have succeeded in doing that 100% so far.

Begin reading slowly and concentrate on both the Scriptures and the images that are drawn in your mind. Then, you can begin to recognize the things within yourself and apply truth to your life. You will be changed.

CHAPTER ONE
A FIRM FOUNDATION

||||||||||||||||||||||||||||||||||||||||||||||||||||||||||||||||||||||||||||||||||||||||||||||||||||||||||||||||||||||||||||||||||||||||||||||||||||||||||||||||||||||||||

FIRE! It has so many different attributes. Delightful to destructive, it has a purifying effect. As we review some of these attributes, we can draw parallels to how God works in our lives – how we are warmed by His presence, purified by His word and how sin is destroyed. If we do not allow God to burn up the sin in our lives and purify our hearts, there is an eternal fire. We do not want to be found in it.

We will also look at the different types of fire and examine the characteristics of God and our relationship to Him. This will show us the flaws within ourselves. Through seeing these flaws and recognizing God for who He is, we are better able to function in the reality of Scripture.

> *"¹⁰ According to the grace of God which was given unto me, as a wise master builder I laid a foundation; and another buildeth thereon. But let each man take heed how he buildeth thereon. ¹¹ For other foundation can no man lay than that which is laid, which is Jesus Christ. ¹² But if any man buildeth on the foundation gold, silver, costly stones, wood, hay, stubble; ¹³ each man's work shall be made manifest: for the day shall declare it, because it is revealed in fire;* [a] *and the fire itself shall prove each man's work of what sort it is. ¹⁴ If any man's work shall abide which he built thereon, he shall receive a reward. ¹⁵ If any man's work shall be burned, he shall suffer loss: but he himself shall be saved; yet so as through fire."*
> *(I Corinthians 3:10-15;)*

1

You can see how beautiful fire is when sitting by a fireplace! Fire has warmth that is soothing and lovely, especially when it is cold. But even on a hot summer's day, a campfire can be delightful. The flames dance round and change color and shape. Each peak seems to delight in itself as it raises and lowers or leaps across the adjoining flames. It has a crisp sound caused by the destruction it leaves in its path.

And destructive it can be. In a moment, fire can rage beyond control, driving back man and beast alike, consuming everything in its path. It can be forceful and irrational, roaring off in any direction. Both useful and dangerous, fire must be tended. It needs attention in order to be controlled, and it needs attention to continue to burn.

Fire is not only a tool for man; it is also symbolic of a wide range of human emotions and experiences. We live in a symbolic fire, and that is the fire we must be ever tending, whether it is soothing, passionate, raging or smoldering. The saddest time of all is when the fire of life goes out. Without the fire of life, there is only a hardened, cold person. Unfortunately, this spiritual death can happen long before a body meets physical death. To avoid becoming cold, it is important for us to tend the fire in our hearts. It is in the symbolic fire, the spiritual fire, where we live, grow, and do battle. The battle in our lives can take many different forms, such as alcoholism or drug addiction. It may be living unequally yoked or with an abusive family member (this does not mean continuing in a situation where your physical health is at risk.) It could be caring for someone you love who cannot care for himself; being jobless, having a job you hate or being in such financial debt you cannot see your way out. Perhaps you are living in a marriage in which you feel trapped but want desperately for things to work out. Imagine seeing all the dreams you hoped life to be, shattered through a glass of reality never considered, or living with bitterness and hatred stirred up from the past. The circumstances can be anything, but the battle belongs to the Lord.

With enough time, heat, and pressure, a piece of coal becomes a diamond. Like a diamond, let us learn how our lives can be created in the image of God.

PERSONAL EXPERIENCE

I have always said that I was saved at the age of 16 in a little Nazarene Church in Texas. But now I realize it was only at that age I began to understand the invitation of Jesus Christ, to accept Him and put my name in the Lamb's book of life. I was saved somewhere between the ages of eight and eleven. I do not remember exactly how old I was, but I remember it was not in a church, but in a movie theater. When I was young, my brother and I would go to the local theater every Saturday. For six Pepsi bottle caps, you could get into the matinee, so of course, everyone was there. There was always a line down the front and around the side of the building, but we would wait.

This one day, there was a Billy Graham movie showing. I do not remember the name or even what the movie was about. All I remember is that it touched my heart. At the end, there was an invitation for anyone who wanted to give his or her life to Christ. I knew then that I wanted what Billy Graham had talked about. It was at that point where the many seeds God had planted in my life began to grow. That was my day of salvation.

My Heart Melts

My heart melts away
at the sight of your pain
The infirmities you have,
every loss, every gain
Selfish corruption,
greed and distain
Bring consequences
that cause heartbreak and shame
Angers expressed
and needless despair
Are what people
can see through and share
But my heart melts
as I see in your eyes
The reflection of hurt
you so well disguise
So I laid down my life
and hung it on a cross
Because my heart melts
when I see the lost.

QUESTIONS TO PONDER

1. What is your foundation for life?

   _____

   _____

2. Can you tell your Salvation story?

   _____

   _____

3. When do you allow your heart to grow cold?

   _____

   _____

4. Where were you when you began to understand God's voice?

   _____

   _____

5. What is your personal spiritual battle?

   _____

   _____

6. Why do you battle?

    _____

    _____

7. What is the fire in your life?

    _____

    _____

8. Is that fire positive or negative?

    _____

    _____

9. How can you make it better?

    _____

    _____

10. Are you warmed daily by your meditation on God's word?

    _____

    _____

CHAPTER TWO
FIRE'S ATTRIBUTES

||||||||||||||||||||||||||||||||||||||||||||||||||||||||||||||||||||||||||||||||||||||||||||||||||||||||||||||||||||||||||||||||||||

TECHNICALLY SPEAKING

First, we want to examine the physical attributes of fire. You will see there is a spiritual message mirrored in each facet, and as we examine the Scriptures, perhaps you can see your reflection.

In the online article *How Fire Works*,[i] author Tom Harris best explains fire:

"Earth, water and air are all forms of matter – they are made up of millions and millions of atoms collected together. Fire isn't matter at all. It's a visible, tangible side effect of matter *changing form* ...."[2]

It is fascinating that Harris so specifically identifies fire as something other than matter. Similarity, the physical attributes of fire reflect God's purpose for placing us in a spiritual inferno – also to "change form." God is not content with us staying as we are. His purpose in our life is to help us know Him more fully and be more like Him. To do that, we must change. We must change our way of thinking and our reactions. This change is not done once and held for eternity. We are continually changing to become more like Jesus.

To have fire, you must have three elements: heat, fuel and oxygen. Without all three elements, fire cannot exist. The source of heat or fuel can change, but oxygen is the one constant. If you take away oxygen, the fire goes out. If we compare that to our lives, we see the one thing that never changes is God. He is the one constant. Our circumstances can change and our feelings or emotions about something can change, but God does not and He, like the oxygen in our atmosphere, is always present.

Fire produces three by-products: smoke, char and ash. Smoke is a reaction produced by the gases that are released. Char is pure carbon;

it is the fuel with the smoke gone. Ash is what you have left that will not burn up. When we consider ourselves as the by-product of God's consuming fire, we see a reaction (smoke), our emotional response to the circumstances around us; and our being, the basic element (char) that is heated and that spirit within us that is left. I am reminded of the Scripture reading in Genesis 3:19 that states, *"... for dust thou art, and unto dust shalt thou return..."* When all else is gone, we are left with our spirit. God's purpose is that our Spirit will be a beautiful reflection of Him.

Fire also produces light, which is a result of carbon atoms being heated. The amazing thing about those carbon atoms burning up is that they can collect on their surroundings. Jesus tells us that we are to be a light to the world. We are to go out and shine. What we do not always realize is the impact this has on our surroundings. If we shine the love of Christ, those around us are impacted.

Harris further notes in his article *How Fire Works* that the chemical reaction in fire is self-perpetuating, as long as fuel and oxygen are available because the flame provides the ignition point.

"... with heat providing the necessary energy, atoms in one gaseous compound break their bonds with each other and recombine with available oxygen atoms in the air to form new compounds plus lots more heat. "[2]

I find these attributes of fire most interesting. As long as we are available, God will provide the energy because God's power is always available. I can hear you saying, "But if the oxygen is removed, the fire goes out!" I must ask, "Do you live in a vacuum?" God is omnipresent. That means He is ALWAYS present. No matter the circumstances. We burn out when we cut ourselves off from God or His purpose for our life.

Now, look at the idea that bonds are broken. We continually seek to break the bonds of many things – bonds with addictions, cares, people, or negative thoughts. This shows us that it is a natural occurrence in the fire. In God's refining fire, those addictions, cares, and circumstances surrounding our lives are broken. Relationships are broken. We see repeatedly how people come and go in our lives. Some influence us more than others. Some have relationships that are harder to break than others. Some relationships last a lifetime.

Here are a few more facts from Harris' article that we can mirror to our walk with God and his fire in our lives:

"Different flammable fuels catch fire at different temperatures. ... The necessary heat level varies depending on the nature of the molecules that make up the fuel."

"The fuel's **size** also affects how easily it will catch fire. A larger fuel ... can absorb a lot of heat, so it takes a lot more energy ..."

"... the fuel's reaction with oxygen may happen very quickly, or it may happen more slowly."

"Thin pieces of fuel burn more quickly than larger pieces because a larger proportion of their mass is exposed to oxygen at any moment."

"... fires from different fuels are like different species of animal – they all behave a little differently. Experts can often figure out how a fire started by observing how it affected the surrounding areas. A fire from a fast-burning fuel that produces a lot of heat will inflict a different sort of damage than a slow-burning, low-heat fire."[1]

KEEPING THE FAITH

> [1]*"Now faith is assurance of things hoped for, a conviction of things not seen. [2] For therein the elders had witness borne to them. [3] By faith we understand that the worlds have been framed by the word of God, so that what is seen hath not been made out of things which appear." (Hebrews 11:1-3)*

Different fuels, sizes and sources will burn differently. So, it is true with us. We each have different personalities and we have different breaking points, strengths, and circumstances.

Just as twigs ignite and burn faster than tree branches, all people do not react in the same manner to God. When we have a spotty prayer life, no real knowledge of Scripture or a weak relationship with Christ, we are quickly consumed – just like a twig. To go from being kindling to a log of fuel, a strong faith is important. Our spiritual growth comes from prayer and our study of Scripture. We need to know not just that God is the Creator of our universe and our Savior, but His character, His desires, and His voice.

Also, as we mature and grow in Christ, it may take greater measures to produce change in our lives, thus greater trials and greater blessings. Sometimes, our initial reaction can be quite volatile to change. We do not like it! We do not want it! We are just fine the way we are! But Christ is always refining us, always wanting us to grow in faith and influence. And He has to treat each of us differently according to our personality, circumstances, needs, and maturity.

Holding onto your faith in the midst of the fire can be tough. But through the challenge, day after day, month after month, and year after year, you gain strength. It is that hope that you must fan to a flame when circumstances seem to drown you.

> [5] *"and hope putteth not to shame; because the love of God hath been shed abroad in our hearts through the Holy Spirit which was given unto us." (Romans 5:5)*

Christ is our hope. The importance of Scripture cannot ever be emphasized enough for it is where we receive our strength and promises and hope. The Scriptures are our safety net. When we are not watching where we are going, we can walk right off the edge or be pushed so far that we lose our balance. That net catches us and keeps us from crashing. The times that we do crash, when we feel our safety net is not in place, we must not forget to continue trusting God to pick us up again. For He will. He is faithful. No matter the circumstances, God will take us through them. I know. He has me again and again.

It is important for us to remember that we are not alone in our struggles; there is often someone else who has been through a similar challenge. Remember, Solomon said, "There is nothing new under the sun."[3] So, many times, we want to insulate ourselves to avoid hurt. In truth, we are only isolating ourselves, which can bring heartache and depression and only compounds our circumstances. When we have others to lean on and encourage us (especially with Scripture), it gives us an accountability that is helpful. It is difficult to see the truth in the midst of despair. Pain can darken the eyes of our memory while a friend can enlighten our hearts through the truth of God's word.

I want to take a moment and caution those who are being the light of the world to someone. Please remember to let the light of love from the Holy Spirit shine through you. Be sure you listen not only to your friend but listen for God's still, small voice before you give advice. You never know the length, depth or height of an individual's heart or what God may be taking them through. So many times, I want to help God. I sometimes ask myself, "Why not then? That was a perfect opportunity!" Often, there is just silence, and sometimes, He softy answers my heart with, "Not now, I am in control." So, your part may not be to give advice. Your part may just be to listen, to be a shoulder to cry on or a friend to just be present.

We are not perfect, but we do have the resources to live a victorious life when we fight our battles. To draw the necessary strength, we have to live by faith and not by sight. We must be living by the Word of God and not the circumstances surrounding us. If we do this, our safety net is always in place. Sometimes, our perception of our distance from it is what is skewed. My greatest desire is to encourage others to live by the grace of God because I truly know, it is sufficient!

It is not our own strength that gets us through. It is not our own wisdom or manipulation that shapes our lives. It is God who created this universe, and He is the one who orchestrates our lives. If we are to see the beauty and unity that brings harmony to us, we must follow the plan written by the Master and emblazoned on our hearts with the Holy Spirit.

PERSONAL EXPERIENCE

There were many seeds of faith planted in my life. When I was a child, there was never a situation where my mother did not say, "God will take care of us." And, of course, He always did. He took care of us every time a project ended, and my dad needed a job at the aerospace company where he worked. And when it looked as if my dad would be called overseas after the ship, U.S. Pueblo was captured by North Korea in 1968 during the Vietnam war, again God took care of us.

Growing up, Sundays were also an important time for devotion and reverence for the Lord. My family went to church on Sundays. Sure, we missed now and then, but even when we visited with relatives on a weekend, we would go to their church. There was never a question about Sunday being devoted to the Lord and that it was a day of rest. There was never a question of whether you would attend church. We spent time together on Sundays. We went to church and then out to eat as a family. It was a relaxing time.

Another great part of building my spiritual life occurred every August in the Davis Mountains of west Texas, where my brother and I would spend a week with my grandmother at a church camp. I think my brother mostly enjoyed climbing the mountain, but I enjoyed all the church services and eating under the big tents set up around camp. People from all denominations came together in the Davis Mountains to worship: Methodist, Baptist, Catholic. Everyone had services.

My grandmother had a small trailer that sat at the bottom of the hill. On Saturday night before everyone started home on Sunday, the entire camp had a closing ceremony on the side of the hill. There was a large white cross, and that night it was lit up. Everyone stood with candles, and I remember what a beautiful sight it was. It was a celebration climax for a week of worship.

Those many seeds of faith have grown a lot over the years. They had good roots by the time I married, which was important since I was only married a week when my husband was deployed overseas with the military. I was to follow as soon as the paperwork was completed. Well, governments have a way of changing the plans of individuals, and it took more than five months for me to join my husband.

In the years that followed, there have been many times that my circumstances have depended upon my faith to carry me through. And seeds of faith continue to be planted and grow in my life. It is never too late for faith to begin, for we always awaken to a new day. The circumstances and people that have been planted in my life are different from yours. Scripture tells us that God's word does not go out void.[4] All those times you have encouraged someone or been encouraged may be the seeds that will grow faith.

PRACTICAL APPLICATION

There are physical laws that we study in science (gravity makes things fall) and math (2 + 2 = 4) that remain constant. You can slice a pie into eight pieces, but there is still only one pie. There may be many ways to slice things up, but the physical laws still apply.

There are spiritual laws, too. God laid down principles in His word that work. We often hear about "karma." Well, what scripture tells us in Galatians 6:7 is:

> *"Be not deceived; God is not mocked: for whatsoever a man soweth, that shall he also reap."*

This is one of those principles. It is recognized by those who do not know God. They call it "karma." Spiritual laws are studied through Scripture and prayer. If you try to go against these principles, you will run into trouble. God set these principals in motion, and they work both positively and negatively in our lives. Use them to your benefit. Learn how God's laws function and how to function within their structure.

> *"[15] Give diligence to present thyself approved unto God, a workman that needeth not to be ashamed, handling aright the word of truth." (II Timothy 2:15)*

In order to present yourself and correctly handle the word of truth, you must get into the word and study it. You must read and spend some time not only in personal Bible study and meditation but in group Bible study. Ask the questions and seek the answers. And as you seek to find the answers for life in the word of truth, you will fan the flame of God's love in your own heart. God sees you differently than you see yourself.

It is all about relationship. Seek to know Him, not only His word. Trust in the word, even in the midst of people who scream at you that things are different from what the word of truth says. Will you be discouraged? Yes. But when you learn perseverance, you will see the hand of God. Will you be hurt? Be assured! But pain reminds us that we are only human and that there is a God much bigger than ourselves. Will you be able to endure? Absolutely! God's grace is sufficient, and His desire is to refine you in His image – not your own expectations.

Sufficient Grace

Between reality and insanity
In the state of confusion
Chaos engulfs me with each new crisis
Flooding life with intrusions

Time sweeps past appearing allusive
Trying to steal my peace.

Sweet peace
Nestled in my soul
The calm like a glassy sea
Embraces my heart.

While complications arise around me
I want to cry out "Cease"

The pressure could surly crush me
But victory is at hand
God says No weapon formed will prosper
All I must do is stand!

So, I'll follow the narrow road
Watching each step I take
And as the trials bombard me
I'll stand in Sufficient Grace.

QUESTIONS TO PONDER

1. Considering the connections, we have already drawn between fire and our own lives. How do you see these aspects of fire in your life?

   _____

   _____

2. What heats you up?

   _____

   _____

3. How quickly do you respond?

   _____

   _____

4. What reactions do you have to circumstances?

   _____

   _____

5. What reactions do you have to people?

   _____

   _____

6. What reactions do you have to God?

_____

_____

7. How do you differentiate insulation from isolation?

_____

_____

8. Do you depend on others to study scripture and tell you what they know?

_____

_____

9. Do you value scripture knowledge over a personal relationship with God?

_____

_____

10. What does a personal relationship with God look like?

_____

_____

CHAPTER THREE
COVENANT

||||||||||||||||||||||||||||||||||||||||||||||||||||||||||||||||||||||||||||||||||||||||||||||||||||||||||||||||||||||||||||||||||||

Let us begin looking at the Scriptures and what they have to say about us. The covenant between Abram and God is first.

> "*¹⁷ And it came to pass, that, when the sun went down, and it was dark, behold, a smoking furnace, and a flaming torch that passed between these pieces. ¹⁸ In that day Jehovah made a covenant with Abram, saying, Unto thy seed have I given this land, from the river of Egypt unto the great river, the river Euphrates:*" (Genesis 15:17-18)

A covenant is usually a binding agreement between two parties. In our society today, we have contracts. Let us look at the scripture above and see how God makes covenant with us. The covenant that was made was not between God and Abram. God gave it to Abram[5]. As a matter of fact, while God "cut" covenant with Abram, Abram was asleep. As Abram slept, God gave him the progression of events (or terms of the agreement) and the promise before He sealed the covenant. God promised Abram descendants, deliverance from oppression and a great land. This was God giving His word. The mutual agreement in this covenant was Abram's responsibility to act on faith in a manner congruent with the agreement. He had to have faith that God would perform.

According to *Vine's Expository Dictionary of Old and New Testament Words,*

> "The word 'covenant' in its sense of an agreement on the part of each of two contracting parties, cannot apply to a covenant between God and man. His covenant is essentially a matter of grace on His part. In contrast to

the covenants made by God are those between men ...
where an oath was taken by both parties."[6]

I both agree and disagree with this statement. The provision and
fulfillment of the covenant is God's responsibility. Just like fire needs
fuel, oxygen and heat, there are three elements to the covenant. First is
the word or promise God gives. Second is trusting in that word, and
third is the action taken for the covenant to be fulfilled. God made the
provision for the completion of His word. Abram had not only to believe
but to act on his belief.

When we look at Abram's life, we see it was not just an easy, laid
back and fun-filled time. It was an adventure, and Abram did not always
do right. In the story of Abram, you will find that he and Sarah did just
exactly what we do, all too often. Instead of resting in the provision of
God, they tried to help God and they doubted. They allowed circum-
stances to dictate their thinking about what God had said.

If you remember from Scripture, Abram and Sarah were quite elderly
when God established His covenant. They were past childbearing years –
they were in their 60s and 70s! Naturally, they couldn't comprehend that
Sarah could give Abram any descendants, especially since she had always
been barren. By the time Isaac, the promised child, was born Abram
was 100 years old. Sarah was 90! How would you like to be chasing a
toddler at that age?

The first mistake this couple made was to doubt. They assumed the
physical barriers were a problem for God and that they needed to help.
Sarah gave her handmaiden to her husband, and he fathered a child
with the servant. But this was not the child of promise. It was not the
fulfillment of God's covenant. This was an illegitimate substitution for
God's provision.

This first-born of Abram brought difficulties into their lives. While
waiting on the promise of God, Abram traveled through the desert and
into Egypt. He was forced to cast his first-born son and the boy's mother
out of his household. Later, Abram was tested and even had to be willing
to sacrifice Isaac, the son of promise. (We will discuss this further when

we get to testing.) But he showed himself a man of great faith and trusted in God, and every promise of the covenant was fulfilled.

Abram and Sarah had to act in a physical manner congruent with God's promise or Isaac could not have been born. The Holy Spirit could have moved upon Sarah as he did with the Virgin Mary years later, but that would not have fulfilled the promise of Abram's seed. God is going to stand true to his promise. Therefore, this old couple had to come together for Abram's seed to produce the child God promised them.

We are much the same way. We believe what God has told us, but our impatience pushes us forward to "help" Him with what he has promised. Resting in faith is alright for short periods of time, but we do not want to be stuck there too long. We are an impatient people. Through modern technology we have learned to look for quick answers. Our fast-food, instant-solution society has us programmed for immediacy. If we have to wait for what we perceive as too long in faith, we will try to do things by our own efforts. However, it is important to remember that God's grace is never received by our efforts. His promises are never fulfilled through our struggling for completion. Just like Abram, we can create an illegitimate substitution that can cause us complications.

LIVING THE WORD

The word "firepot" in the passage from Genesis means oven. As I understand it, it is an oven of intense heat. I image it as a kiln, like artisans use to fire pottery. Kilns reach extreme temperatures, much hotter than the oven in your kitchen. And this particular "firepot" was smoking so we know it produced a great deal of heat.

But Genesis did not mention just the firepot – a blazing torch accompanied it. Although you might imagine the torch blazing beneath the firepot to keep it hot, I imagine it as cutting a path that the firepot follows, a flame that directs the path. This is a perfect picture of just how God uses the Holy Spirit to direct our path while Christ burns within our hearts. This is how we learn from God's covenant with Abram.

When God makes a covenant, there is no doubt. Just as God was specific in His covenant with Abraham, He is specific with you and me. It is His word, His promise, His obligation.

> *"[16] For men swear by the greater: and in every dispute of theirs the oath is final for confirmation. [17] Wherein God, being minded to show more abundantly unto the heirs of the promise the immutability of his counsel, interposed with an oath; [18] that by two immutable things, in which it is impossible for God to lie, we may have a strong encouragement, who have fled for refuge to lay hold of the hope set before us:" (Hebrews 6:16-18)*

It would be very difficult for me to see, believe or understand Abram if he stood before me at 100 years old with a 90-year-old wife telling me that God was going to give them a child. I might imagine an adoption but never a live birth. But Abram knew what God had promised and the circumstances did not change that.

As people who live under grace, we have a new covenant – the covenant Jesus Christ makes with us. When speaking of the new covenant, the writer of Hebrews says in Chapter 8, Verse 10, *"For this is the covenant that I will make with the house of Israel. After those days, saith the Lord; I will put my laws into their mind, and on their heart also will I write them: And I will be to them a God, And they shall be to me a people:"*

PERSONAL EXPERIENCE

As someone who has accepted a relationship with Jesus, I know that God has made a covenant with me. His promise is that I am someone who He calls His own. He has, is, and will continue to write His law on my heart and in my mind so that I may know Him better.

But that is not the only covenant God has given me. I, too, have a promise from the Lord. You may not be able to see it or understand it, but He has given me a great encouragement. My promise is one of salvation, peace and harmony. And although I have not received peace in the way I expected it, I have received it. Harmony has crept into my life slowly and washed away many stresses. I have not seen the complete fulfillment, but I know it is coming because God game me His word. This promise has held my faith and kept me looking ahead. I cannot say that I have not looked behind me. But looking back does not keep my eyes on God's promise. I've tried to help God out, but reaped consequences that only complicated things. The covenant I have is true. It is a promise that is consistent with the word and from the word. That is important to remember.

Let me make a side note here. Being <u>consistent</u> with Scripture is as important as a message coming <u>from</u> the Scripture. It is possible to take Scripture and make it say what you want but that might not be consistent with what God is saying. We do not want to take things out of context. I know a Biblical scholar's interpretation of this Scripture would not render a personal conclusion, but because of the manner it was given to me, my prayer requests at that time in my life and its consistency with Scripture I know it is a promise from God.

I believe it is important for you to know just how I know with such certainty that my promise is to be fulfilled. It is a message that God gave me during church one Sunday morning.

I was praising with my heart and soul that morning. I do not often have such vivid pictures during my worship time but on that day I envisioned Jesus riding into Jerusalem on a donkey. I am sure such vivid impressions should happen much more often and I am sure it is my own disconnectedness from worship that is the reason it does not. This particular day, it was powerful and wonderful. Worship was alive and vibrant. And the presence of the Living God was manifest. Not manifest in something that you could touch or see but his presence was very real. Just like when you are all alone and then you "feel" someone else is there and you turn and sure enough, someone is. God's presence was that way. I could feel it.

The Scripture tells us that God inhabits the praises of his people. This particular day, He inhabited my world. As we sang "Hosanna" during worship, I pictured Christ entering Jerusalem on a donkey and the crowds of people waving palm branches and tossing them before Him shouting, "Hosanna to the King," praising the Savior and giving honor and glory to the one who had come to deliver them from oppression.

The worship portion ended, and as the service continued, a thought went galloping through my mind: "Zechariah 9:9." This was not my thought. It was one that invaded my thoughts. So, I grabbed my Bible. I did not grab my Bible because I knew God had just given me a wonderful word. No, I sat there with a huge question "Is Zechariah a book in the Bible?" I went straight to the index to find out. Yep! It was there. Then after, I questioned where? and if there were even 9 chapters in Zechariah? I began to read. *"Rejoice greatly, O Daughter of Zion! Shout, Daughter of Jerusalem! See, your king comes to you, righteous and having salvation, gentle and riding on a donkey."* (NIV)

I was startled with the realization that God had inhabited my morning worship. I had envisioned only moments before our Lord riding triumphantly into Jerusalem on a donkey. It could only have been the Lord knowing my heart and my mind and bringing affirmation.

That verse and the verses that follow spoke deep to my heart because they affirmed to me the promise of salvation, peace and harmony I was praying for in my life and the lives of others.

The Holy Spirit blazed through my mind, and God cut covenant with me that day. I was not asleep like Abram. I was simply dazed. It is a promise that Jesus has seared on my heart and mind to remind me that I am loved. I cannot do anything to fulfill that promise and I cannot do anything to void it. I cannot hurry it along or slow it down. It is the fire of my faith for my family and for myself. If I am discouraged by circumstances, I can read that verse and it tells me from the beginning to rejoice. If ever I doubt, it, reminds me that God sees me and knows me. He cares for everything in our lives, and He cared enough to give me a wonderful promise. If I am impatient, I read Zechariah 9:12 that says, *"12 Turn you to the stronghold, ye prisoners of hope: even today do I declare that I will render double unto thee"* So even if I feel trapped and hopeless, the truth is that EVEN NOW God is here.

I am not unique or any more special to God than anyone else. Like everyone else, I have had my doubts and tried to hurry things along. I have argued with God, and pleaded with Him, tried to help Him and waited upon Him. And through it all, Jesus has shown me how I need to change to be more like Him.

I am no more loved or forgiven than anyone else, including you. I am only encouraged because God has shown me experientially that He cares for me. He has given me a hope and a future. That means I am still struggling with every breath to learn more of how to please God and be more like Jesus.

Just as God gave my promise to me, I know that He has a promise for your life. Just as He has a plan and purpose for me, He has one for you. Have you accepted the promise of eternal life through salvation? It begins there. It is with God's people that He makes His covenant. It is with those that He calls His own that He will put His laws in their minds and write them on your hearts.

If you have not accepted the promise of eternal life, open wide your heart and trust God. Allow Jesus to burn within you. He will burn up the sin in your life and take away the heavy burden of guilt. Like gaining weight, you do not realize just how heavy your load is until it is removed. Invite Jesus into your life.

Do not silence Him in your heart. Allow Him to work through your life. There are so many people in our society and churches today who think they can hold Jesus just in their hearts and turn to Him only in times of trouble. You must give Him your heart AND your life to develop the relationship He wants with you.

> *"23 And he said unto all, If any man would come after me, let him deny himself, and take up his cross daily, and follow me. 24 For whosoever would save his life shall lose it; but whosoever shall lose his life for my sake, the same shall save it. 25 For what is a man*

*profited, if he gain the whole world, and lose or for-
feit his own self?* [26] *For whosoever shall be ashamed
of me and of my words, of him shall the Son of man
be ashamed, when he cometh in his own glory, and
the glory of the Father, and of the holy angels.* [27] *But I
tell you of a truth, There are some of them that stand
here, who shall in no wise taste of death, till they see
the kingdom of God. (Luke 9:23-27)*

There Is A Flame A Burning

There is a flame a burning
Burning within my heart.
It is the flame that burns up my sin
The flame that ignites my passion for life

There is a flame a burning
Burning within my mind
It is the flame that destroys shame
The flame that purifies my desires

There is a flame a burning
Burning within my soul
It is the flame that sanctifies
It is the Holy Spirit to teach me

There is a flame a burning
Burning within my eyes
It is the flame that shines
The flame that bring light to others

There is a flame a burning
Burning within my hands
It is the flame that reaches out to others
The flame that heals body, mind and spirit

There is a flame a burning
Burning within me
It is the flame of Jesus
The fire of the Spirit, the torch of God

QUESTIONS TO PONDER

1. Have you accepted the promise of eternal life through salvation?

   _____

   _____

2. What covenant do you have in your life?

   _____

   _____

3. Does God have your cooperation?

   _____

   _____

4. Do you give your heart, your mind and your soul to worshiping God?

   _____

   _____

5. When do you worship God?

   _____

   _____

6. How do you display your faith?

_____

_____

7. Do you move forward in patience or impatience?

_____

_____

8. Do you try to help God in His promises?

_____

_____

9. Do you place limits or restrictions on a covenant with God?

_____

_____

10. Have you experienced consequences because of your response to God's covenant with you?

_____

_____

11. Is anyone else involved in your covenant? If so, who?

_____

_____

12. How can you demonstrate cooperation with God's covenant?

_____

_____

CHAPTER FOUR
CONSUMING FIRE

||||||||||||||||||||||||||||||||||||||||||||||||||||||||||||||||||||||||||||||||||||||||||||||||||||||||||||||||||||

"23 The sun was risen upon the earth when Lot came unto Zoar. 24 Then Jehovah rained upon Sodom and upon Gomorrah brimstone and fire from Jehovah out of heaven; 25 and he overthrew those cities, and all the Plain, and all the inhabitants of the cities, and that which grew upon the ground. 26 But his wife looked back from behind him, and she became a pillar of salt. 27 And Abraham gat up early in the morning to the place where he had stood before Jehovah: 28 and he looked toward Sodom and Gomorrah, and toward all the land of the Plain, and beheld, and, lo, the smoke of the land went up as the smoke of a furnace.

29 And it came to pass, when God destroyed the cities of the Plain, that God remembered Abraham, and sent Lot out of the midst of the overthrow, when he overthrew the cities in which Lot dwelt." (Genesis 19:23-29)

Our next sight of fire is again in Genesis, and it deals with disobedience and sin. I find it interesting that this fire that came to destroy what was wrong in the land was a burning sulfur. Sulfur is a fire that must burn itself out.

All too often today, we do not want to acknowledge the fact that there are consequences for what we do. Like Adam and Eve, we want to blame someone else. There is always an excuse. "It was the way they were brought up. You cannot blame them!" "If so-and-so- hadn't told me it was alright I never would have done it." "No one told me that would happen." "When I was younger..."

However, there are consequences for actions! Even if you were a victim at one time or someone else said something contrary to God's word was acceptable, you are responsible for what you do and say. God has set down spiritual principles that we are to live our lives by and when those are violated, it is called sin. It does not matter what society says or what is politically correct or how we feel about something; a violation of God's law is sin. We might feel that it does not seem "fair", but God did not create us for "fairness". We were created for Him and He cannot and will not tolerate sin.

The way man perceives something, or the way society reacts to circumstances does not mean that it is right. What man thinks is right can be very wrong in the eyes of God.

Unfortunately, we have gotten away from drawing boundaries and saying that things are right or wrong. We have thrown out a standard of living and have lowered expectations, so we can feel good about ourselves. We have tried to eliminate shame from our thinking. The reality is that accomplishments, work ethics and achievements are things that make us feel good about ourselves. When a standard is raised for us to rise up and meet, we earn a sense of accomplishment and a boost to our self-esteem. Lowering expectations and standards actually leaves us with a sense of failure and a loss of self-esteem.

Lowering standards to accommodate shame is apparently what had been done in Sodom and Gomorrah. People were living their lives in sin and tolerating others to remain in sin in their society. They pushed God's standards to the side and denied or ignored consequences to their actions.

It is important that we deal with the disobedience and sin that exists in our lives. God does not ask us to change to come to Him. But once we have accepted His covenant of salvation, it is easy to begin to see our own self-destruction. After accepting the gift of salvation, we can then choose to live in destruction or begin to follow righteousness.

Notice, I did not say the destruction was something that someone else did to us or put us in or gave us permission to follow. We are responsible for our own actions. We are born into sin and the bad things that happen to us are all part of our decaying world. No matter what circumstances we have lived in or through, we can choose to change our circumstances. It may not be an easy process or a quick one, but as I once heard someone say, "little things make big things happen".

Remember, God's plan is that we have life abundantly.[7] How can we have an abundant life if we are destroying it at every turn? It is God's responsibility to show us our unrighteousness and provide an example of righteousness. It is our responsibility to walk in righteousness. God did not create puppets. He will not overstep the free will He gave us. God created men to think and choose.

As we look at sin, we must also look at the aspects of the fire which deal with revelation of God's love and grace. Look at the story of Sodom and Gomorrah being destroyed.

Sin was rampant, and God could no longer tolerate such blatant disobedience. As is always true with God's grace, He forewarns of disaster in hopes of repentance. God wants to abound grace, not destruction. It is His desire that all be saved. At the same time, He does not override the free will He has placed in man. Therefore, with no repentance in sight, He rained burning sulfur down and destroyed the cities. I imagine the stench of burnt sulfur is far better to God than the stench of our sin.

Sulfur is not a fire that can be extinguished with water. It must burn up. The people of Sodom and Gomorrah were unwilling to turn to God and were militant in their disobedience. But even in the face of this destruction, God showed His grace and mercy. There was but one righteous man in the city and God delivered him before He rained down destruction upon the sinful. Lot was able to take his family and flee to a nearby town.

But as is true with many of us, Lot's wife could not keep her eyes from looking back and she was turned into a pillar of salt. If we continue to desire the past with some hope in our heart, we are unable to move forward. I believe Lot's wife was doing just that. I believe she hoped that some could escape the destruction. Her heart was obviously tender for her neighbors and friends, and I believe she wanted their life to be saved. But when God calls us to move forward, we cannot look back. When we are in God's grace, we need to be obedient to His word. If we disobey, our progress will be halted.

I believe Lot's wife's compassion is not what destroyed her. Her looking back showed her disobedience. It is that disobedience that destroyed her.

It seems looking back is all too natural. Personally, I have looked over my shoulder far too often and long. It can be paralyzing. Looking back will preserve the pain and not allow you to move forward and to look ahead with hope and faith. A drug addict cannot stay around drug dealers or users and expect to get better. Someone dieting cannot stock their shelves with cake and ice cream and wonder why the scales are going in the wrong direction.

Disobedience to God's laws will always bring destruction! His instruction for family and marriage is for protection and unity. Keeping yourself pure before marriage protects you from disease and a lot of heartbreak. It also protects you from mentally bringing someone else into your marriage bed. As Josh McDowell said, "You never regret sex you did not have."

Monogamy promotes unity. It is sometimes hard enough for two people to agree on how, when and why to do something. When extra partners are brought into a situation, it does not add to the complication, it multiplies it. One husband and one wife plus Jesus is all that a marriage needs for unity. Please note too, that if you take Jesus out of the picture, it can divide the unity. If you doubt this, look at the divorce rate in our society today. We have removed God from our schools, marriages, and lives in general. We see and experience our foundations crumbling. We should not allow illegitimate influences to sway us from God's promises for us.

God's will is for us to be delivered. He always leaves the choice to us. We can choose destruction or grace. All too often we choose destruction over grace. Today our country abounds in destruction through lies, food, gambling, drugs, alcohol, sexual addictions, rioting and more.

We choose immoral behavior over righteousness. The touted doctrines of tolerance and entitlement work to push morality and righteousness to the side. The enemy will wrap up a pretty package to temp and confuse issues in order to entice you to submit to him instead of God. Selfishness and instant gratification are no substitute for God's promises, presence, or provision. Holding out for God's promises and submitting to His timing is far more rewarding.

One of the most volatile issues that clearly shows destruction in our country today is abortion. Women unwilling to accept that a child is a gift from God and a blessing will accept the destruction of their own child in their womb. There are a great number of reasons that they will use to justify their action; financials, family, outside pressure or simple acceptance of today's societal solution that an unwanted pregnancy is best handled with abortion. The truth that life is precious, and that adoption is an excellent solution, are concepts that have been stigmatized because they can be difficult. Selfishness says take the easy road. It does not tell you that what appears to be the easy road has complications and consequences later.

One Saturday before Mother's Day years ago, I was involved in helping set up the "Cemetery of the Innocence". This cemetery consists of crosses and stars of David set up in surveyed rows to represent a number of abortions. It is a memorial for each child who has died. Wreaths and flowers are placed periodically throughout to represent the mothers who are victimized by abortion and die at the hands of abortionists. The horror of women dying from abortion has not changed just because it is legal.

Setting up on concrete on a windy day gave us a lot of trouble. Our stands kept blowing over and it seemed we spent more time doing repairs than we did in prayer. But as I peered out over the crosses, and as I listened to the testimonies of girls affected by abortion, I began to understand.

Webster's definition for *abortion* is: *to miscarry; to fail to come to fruition.*

Abortion is a direct attack on the cross. God's greatest gift is the gift of life He gave to us through Jesus on the cross. Abortion strikes out against life before it has a chance to come to fruition.

The struggles these mothers go through in trying to make a decision is heart wrenching. It is an unnecessary, heartbreaking, choice that we have given them. There was a time that these mothers, most very young, did not have to decide between life and death. They choose only between how and who would care for their child. Because of the hardness of men's hearts, our attitude now is one that expects them to choose death for their child rather than for someone else to love it. There is no choice. Consideration of living is not considered a choice.

It is not just the death of the child that occurs in abortion. When any child dies, a part of the mother dies. The testimony of the women who have experienced abortion was that abortion brings great amounts of guilt and shame along with it.

It draws you away from the fact that God's gift of children to us is a precious blessing. Today people are laughed at and belittled if they have several children. For several decades' society expected you to have one or two children and then stop. Three was pushing it and how could you think of having more?! Most assuredly you should never have children until it is convenient and affordable. This attitude is changing our society. The idea of being a stay-at-home mom now holds a stigmatism.

However, God speaks of many children in a family in Psalm 127:5 *"Happy is the man that hath his quiver full of them: They shall not be put to shame, When they speak with their enemies in the gate."* I pray that we again turn to God and believe that our children are a precious blessing from God and that we can trust in Him to fulfill His promises in our lives. If we can learn that it is all we need to know to stop the tragic deaths of our aborted children.

Here is one of the big differences between God's laws and the laws of man. It is the difference between offense and defense. God's laws are on the side of offense. They are set down to protect man from the harmful consequences of his actions. Man sets down laws of defense to correct the consequences of his destructive behavior. Ironically, if we would all follow God's Ten Commandments, man's laws would be unnecessary.

It is obvious that we are living in a selfish and disobedient society. The generation of "baby boomers" rioted, protested, and argued its way through the legal system and brought about reform that says you can choose for yourself what is right or wrong. Subsequent generations have added the idea that if you do not think my way then you should keep it to yourself. The attitude is one that they do not want to be bothered with anything contrary to their own small world and stand back if you dare to intrude! We now have a generation of "millennials" demanding everything, contributing little to nothing, and intolerant of anyone who does not think their way. This destructive thinking has morphed into a "my way or no way" attitude.

The truth is that no man is an island. The selfish principles that society is calling their "rights!!!" are opposite to the laws of God and have brought a greater demand for man's law. The boomers that rioted for government out of their lives has brought on the greatest demand for government intrusion. The millennials have taken it a step further and are demanding socialism without having been taught the consequences. Chaos, hate, rioting and destruction are the consequences of accepting sin over grace. Like allowing the nose of the camel in the tent, soon you have the entire camel.

We are reaping the consequences of a selfish attitude. As retirement is upon the "baby boomers", the generations that follow expect everything to be given to them. Youth today are rude, impatient, and demanding. Crime, sex, and violence are parts of the lives of children through movies, cartoons, television and the abuse they experience in their families. All the while, they are wondering why their parents and grandparents are so oppressive. Parents and grandparents are wondering why children are so unruly.

The generation that was looking to find itself in the sixties is still looking today. Instead of exploring the country and blaming "the establishment" for all their woes, they now look for themselves through counselors, new age religions, and government assistance. They are still protesting but now they expect "the establishment" to make laws to correct all the problems they helped create. It seems a half century later they would have learned that the laws and government they thought oppressive before are the same or worse as those that now they seek to improve their consequences.

Albert Einstein is credited as saying the definition of insanity is "doing the same thing over and over but expecting different results". I guess that explains why so many are in therapy today. If we would stop looking so hard for ourselves and seek God, we would find more joy than has been experienced in the past decades.

Joy is something our children need. I am saddened each time I see kids today who have more stress in their lives than joy. Have you noticed that so many children do not smile? Where did all these serious faces come from? They are the by-products of a sinful society. Children are expected to act like adults and if they cannot control themselves to do so, they are medicated to fall in line. Or they are beaten and abused to conform. Their lost childhood is sought later. Simple pleasures are ridiculed as "ridiculous". Our teens and pre-teens are engaging in sex and drugs earlier and earlier. Suicide and murder are not remote concepts but have touched the lives of far too many in our society, especially the youth.

I remember how happy we were as kids. When we prayed in school and our parents taught us right from wrong. We enjoyed life! Now our kids are afraid of being shot at school, they are bullied, and committing suicide at an unprecedented rate. Parents and children are in therapy. Sexually Transmitted Diseases (STD's) and Acquired Immune Deficiency Syndrome (AIDS) are epidemic proportions and abortion is used as a form of birth control. Our prisons are filled to overflowing and the age of violent criminals is dropping. Yes, sin abounds across our land, and so does its destruction. It is time to take a serious look at what we are doing.

Gods consuming fire can purify. When gold is refined, it is heated and then the impurities are skimmed off the top. When God refines us, he heats things up and skims the impurities off. When you read about heaven's streets of gold in the book of Revelation, you will notice that they are transparent. Pure gold is transparent. It is the impurity that clouds it, just as impurities cloud our lives.

The sins and impurities of our life cloud our own thinking. Therefore, they must be consumed just like Sodom and Gomorrah were consumed. When Jesus purifies our lives, we become transparent to Him and to others. Although the heat of purification can be extreme and consumes sin, it is necessary for us to be transformed into the image of Christ who knew no sin. God will not abide sin in the land. The righteous will be saved but the sin will be consumed with a fire like sulfur. One that burns extremely hot until it goes out because there is nothing left. Better this process happens within our hearts than we be destroyed by God's judgment.

We must also remember that we cannot look back. When Lots wife turned to see what God had done, she was turned into a pillar of salt. We cannot look back and long for the life we lived before God delivered us out of sin.

That is not always easy. Sin is attractive before it ensnares you. If you could not get a "buzz" or "high" from drugs they would have no appeal. Alcohol can "make you relax" and sex "feels so good." People want to find that rush in life. But they will ever be chasing the rush. Only God can fulfil the need in our hearts.

When we look at sin, we see its appeal, not the snare below the surface. Last time someone offered you a drink did you see the shattered windshield and smashed vehicle with a body? No, you thought about laughter and partying while you drank. Did that chocolate bar give you visions of thunder thighs? Of course not! You felt soothed and comforted as the chocolate melted in your mouth. How about that blonde with the blue eyes? Did you get all itchy from the thought of venereal disease? Or was it more of a tingle that swept over your body as it pulsed, and your heart pounded? Even reading the enticements, it is easy to dismiss the truth of the consequences because sin is first – attractive!

Remember that all of the things I have just mentioned can have a legitimate place. I do not believe drinking is wrong. Jesus himself drank. His first miracle was turning the water into wine at a wedding. However, we are told not to drink to drunkenness. There is a line you should not cross. A drink is not sin. Drunkenness is the sin. For some individuals, that means one drink is more than they can handle. Chocolate is delicious, and studies have shown that dark chocolate has some beneficial qualities that help prevent heart disease. Gluttony is the sin. Sex is something that God made as a great pleasure for a husband and his wife to enjoy and to have children. It is sex outside of marriage, or rape that is sinful and destructive. And continuing in sin ensnares you and brings destruction.

When God delivers you from something, do not look back. It could be your downfall. Just ask the drug addict or the alcoholic or that person on a diet. Look at the teenager trying to raise a baby or that was pulled into prostitution. The victims of sin can be found both dead and dying. Drunk drivers send victims to the morgue daily. Obesity can cause all kinds of health problems. Families are dying from alcoholism, drug addiction, abuse and sexual immorality by the minute. Teen suicide is on the rise and homosexuality has a sea of people dying both physically, emotionally, and spiritually.

Yes, sin is destructive. However, there is a way out. God provided that way. Just like Lot and his family were able to escape from Sodom and Gomorrah, you too can escape the clutches and destruction of sin around you. You must first trust and accept God. You must believe both who He is and what He has said. Accept Christ, listen and obey God's instruction, and you can survive. And if you struggle doing it alone, find someone to help.

There is another fire that does not go out and this fire will not burn itself out. It is the fire of Hell. This is an eternal fire. Some think that death just brings an end; that there is nothing to follow. That is another lie to avoid. You do not want your final destination to be the lake of fire.

Before you put this book down or throw it against the wall, please ask yourself: "If this is wrong, what have I lost?". If there is no Hell or demons; what have you to gain with alcohol, sex, food, and drugs? Are hangovers, addictions, and disease really what will make you happy?

BUT...If I am right and you continue turning away from God, do you want an eternity in hell?

How did you answer the question about salvation? If you could not answer it affirmatively, as we look at the consuming fire, you will want to consider the consequences of your decision.

The ultimate consuming fire is that of Hell. Ever consuming, never extinguished. The fire of Hell is not where you want to be found. Hell, continual pain, torment, isolation and knowing separation from God is the eternal consequence to rejecting Christ. Not only are these things described in scripture, but there are people who have had death experiences that have described these very things. This is a message that you will rarely or never hear in our seeker friendly church sermons today. That is unfortunate because it shows how even the church has cowered to political correctness and shied away from proclaiming sin to be sin and Hell as a consequence.

We have become so comfortable with what society says is permissible that we readily incorporate it in our lives without a thought for God's word. We have become as comfortable with the sin around us that we accept it as normal and right. Instead of holding our lives up to the standard of God's law and rising up to that standard, we have allowed ourselves to slip and be ensnared by the culture around us.

We do not want to appear to be different even though God has called us to be different. We do not want to run away from something that everyone else believes is alright because we might look silly or stupid in their eyes. We want what appears to be the easy road.

When you go to a crowded place or you see a parade on television, there is always someone with a child on their shoulders. That child is raised up where they can see. Unless that child is right in front or raised up, they cannot see what is coming. As adults, unless we sit atop the shoulders of God, or are ahead of the crowd, we cannot see what is coming. We are just in the midst of the crowd, going along with whatever they say. We are being pushed along or our vision blocked by others. Jumping up and down in place to get a glimpse is not going to help. In the midst of that crowd you can be trampled. You have to get out of the crowd.

The alternative to sin and destruction is accepting righteousness. It is a life of relationship with Jesus. It is a covenant with God. It is a life spent following God's laws in order to be blessed by their boundaries. Trusting and believing God will fulfill his promises while you walk by faith. And after an abundant life on earth, you will have an eternity in Heaven. I would encourage you to flee the destruction and follow God in obedience and not look back.

Clouded Vision

I cannot see tomorrow
I will not face it today.
Today there's too much living
For tomorrow's passion to steal away.

Yesterday is behind me.
The past has held much pain
Today I must go on living
While yesterday fades to gray.

Today is all I have
The now is where I will be
Living each day to the fullest
And becoming all I can be.

Sweet memories they can follow
And past lessons I have learned
To give me joy in living,
To make decisions not concerns

Tomorrow is clouded in mystery
Though God's promises are there
I'll wait until they find me
As His fiery passion leads me there

Shades of gray behind me
Cloudy passion ahead
As I press on toward the mark
The Son shines overhead

Questions to Ponder

1. Have you accepted Jesus as your savior?

_____

_____

2. For those who call themselves Christian; how does your life look?

_____

_____

3. What issue do you struggle with or has you ensnared?

_____

_____

4. Are you looking back?

_____

_____

5. Are you looking at your life and wanting to live in it but still be saved from destruction?

_____

_____

6. Are you seeking your own desires or those of God?

_____

_____

7. Would you be the one righteous person found that God would call out of a city He was destroying?

_____

_____

8. Are you helping others to live a righteous life?

_____

_____

9. How can you be a good example? Friend? Mentor?

_____

_____

10. Is there someone you can be accountable to? Are you accountable?

_____

_____

CHAPTER FIVE
TESTING

"22 And it came to pass after these things, that God did prove Abraham, and said unto him, Abraham; and he said, Here am I. ²And he said, Take now thy son, thine only son, whom thou lovest, even Isaac, and get thee into the land of Moriah; and offer him there for a burnt-offering upon one of the mountains which I will tell thee of. ³And Abraham rose early in the morning, and saddled his ass, and took two of his young men with him, and Isaac his son; and he clave the wood for the burnt-offering, and rose up, and went unto the place of which God had told him. ⁴On the third day Abraham lifted up his eyes, and saw the place afar off. ⁵And Abraham said unto his young men, Abide ye here with the ass, and I and the lad will go yonder; and we will worship, and come again to you. ⁶And Abraham took the wood of the burnt-offering, and laid it upon Isaac his son; and he took in his hand the fire and the knife; and they went both of them together. ⁷And Isaac spake unto Abraham his father, and said, My father: and he said, Here am I, my son. And he said, Behold, the fire and the wood: but where is the lamb for a burnt-offering? ⁸And Abraham said, God will [a] provide himself the lamb for a burnt-offering, my son: so they went both of them together.

⁹And they came to the place which God had told him of; and Abraham built the altar there, and laid the wood in order, and bound Isaac his son, and laid

him on the altar, upon the wood. ¹⁰ And Abraham stretched forth his hand, and took the knife to slay his son. ¹¹ And the angel of Jehovah called unto him out of heaven, and said, Abraham, Abraham: and he said, Here am I. ¹² And he said, Lay not thy hand upon the lad, neither do thou anything unto him; for now I know that thou fearest God, seeing thou hast not withheld thy son, thine only son, from me. ¹³ And Abraham lifted up his eyes, and looked, and, behold, behind him a ram caught in the thicket by his horns: and Abraham went and took the ram, and offered him up for a burnt-offering in the stead of his son. ¹⁴ And Abraham called the name of that place [b] Jehovah-jireh: as it is said to this day, In the mount of Jehovah [c] it shall be provided. ¹⁵ And the angel of Jehovah called unto Abraham a second time out of heaven, ¹⁶ and said, By myself have I sworn, saith Jehovah, because thou hast done this thing, and hast not withheld thy son, thine only son, ¹⁷ that in blessing I will bless thee, and in multiplying I will multiply thy seed as the stars of the heavens, and as the sand which is upon the sea-shore; and thy seed shall possess the gate of his enemies; ¹⁸ and in thy seed shall all the nations of the earth [d] be blessed; because thou hast obeyed my voice. ¹⁹ So Abraham returned unto his young men, and they rose up and went together to Beer-sheba; and Abraham dwelt at Beer-sheba."
(Genesis 22:1-19)

When it comes to testing, it is not unusual that we can feel burnt. As we will see here, when testing comes, it does not always seem like God is providing, but that we are going to get burned.

The test we see here with Abraham is a very good example. It was only after Isaac, the son of promise, was bound and placed on the wood as an offering, before the angel of the Lord appeared and stopped him from killing the boy and providing the sacrifice. This shows us that God is not beyond requiring us to go to extremes. The idea that "God wouldn't make me do that!" needs to be discarded from our thinking. God wants us to understand a number of things when we are tested.

First and foremost, we must understand that He Is God! He knows all and is our Creator who wants to reveal things to us. We cannot just give lip service to our faith and not be willing to follow through with what God asks of us. We cannot stop short and say God did not *really* expect me to go that far then expect Him to provide because we place our expectations on Him. God does not want small things from us. He wants to trust us with big things in our lives. To do that, He has to prove to us that we can trust Him; no matter what He asks.

It was no small thing for Abraham to place Isaac on the alter for a sacrifice. The reality was Isaac was the son God gave to Abraham and Sarah; their only son, born in their old age. When your only son is born when you are about 100 years old, it is not logical to think that you will start again. And can you imagine what Sarah would have said or done if Abraham had returned alone? Could she have accepted that her son was sacrificed? Keep in mind too that Sarah had a hard time believing she would ever have a child.

Some might want to interject here that God's promise was to Abraham and not Sarah so she would be justified. It is most important to remember that when you marry, you are spiritually bound together. Two become one flesh. So, the promise, although given to Abraham, was for both him and Sarah. A child comes from two people, not one.

The spiritual reality here was that God had made a promise to Abraham. He not only promised a son, but that he could be the father of many nations. Abraham understands that if God took away what to him appeared to be the fulfillment of that promise, God would still come through and fulfill His word.

We too must understand that we do not always correctly perceive how God intends to fulfill promises, but, He will always come through. We too must follow through with the things God asks us to do. We cannot decide on our own to stop short, assuming God wants us to stop and that He has a different provision. We only stop when He says stop; no matter the price of our sacrifice or the time it takes to be fulfilled.

Grolier's New Book of Knowledge, published in 1972 says that "Tests can help you to know yourself better; to find your gifts, your interest, and your possibilities; and to discover your weaknesses before they can spoil your plans." It also states that "If circumstances make it impossible for you to be in the best form for test taking, do not give up hope. Your reserve of strength will come into play. In fact, some people do their best when the odds are against them."

What a great explanation for what God is doing in our lives. Remember all those tests you took in school? Remember how you looked forward to them? It was not with excitement and joy but with fear and trembling. Tests are used to measure what we know. God's testing in our lives is the same. It shows us just how much we have learned.

There comes a time in all our lives that we have to make a decision. It will not be an easy decision. What you feel, what you see and what you know to be true will all conflict with what God asks of you. But, He will ask a strict obedience to His will. Like Abraham, that test will come before the promise is fulfilled.

> "[17] By faith Abraham, being tried, [a] offered up Isaac: yea, he that had gladly received the promises was offering up his only begotten son; [18] even he [b] to whom it was said, [c] In Isaac shall thy seed be called: [19] accounting that God is able to raise up, even from the dead; from whence he did also in a figure receive him back." (Hebrews 11:17-19)

What I see today is that most of us do not have enough trust in God to believe our hopes can be raised, much less the dead be raised! We walk more by sight than by faith. We are a "show me" people. If we do not see the dead raised, we refuse to believe it could happen. We trust more in science than in the Creator of all things. We are not placing our trust and faith in God. We take our promises and cling to them instead of trusting God for their fulfillment. That is not what God wants for us. He wants us first. Then He will fulfill His promises to us.

We place our expectations on the promises of God and then expect Him to fulfill our expectations. It does not work that way. We are being conformed to an image God has for us. We cannot conform God to our image. Besides, would you really want God to look like you?

Fire has three elements, heat, oxygen and fuel. Fuel can be one of many things, wood, paper, gas, or oil to name a few. Heat can be applied by another fire, by friction or by a short circuit. Without oxygen there would be no fire. Flash point is the temperature at which a particular fuel begins to burn.

The Trinity provides the fire in our lives. We receive our life through God the Father. He is the creator. He gives us the breath of life, our oxygen. Jesus is the fuel. We are fed by His word and by the example He gave us on earth. The Holy Spirit provides us with the heat. He speaks to our hearts and brings convictions to our minds. The flash point in our lives is when we have undergone enough pressure to surrender our will. At that point, God lights the flame of faith to carry us through.

You hear it said, "Don't pray for patience!", but I say to you, pray for patience. It is part of our maturing process. Our tests will be whatever it takes for God to reach into our soul and extract His will. It is His desire that we are transformed into the image of Christ. We can go willingly, or we can take the test over again. God builds upon the lessons already learned.

> "3 seeing that his divine power hath granted unto us all things that pertain unto life and godliness, through the knowledge of him that called us [a]by his own glory and virtue; 4 whereby he hath granted unto us his precious and exceeding great promises; that through these ye may become partakers of [b]the divine nature, having escaped from the corruption that is in the world by lust. 5 Yea, and for this very cause adding on your part all diligence, in your faith

supply virtue; and in your virtue knowledge; [6]and in your knowledge self-control; and in your self-control [c]patience; and in your [d]patience godliness; [7]and in your godliness [e]brotherly kindness; and in your [f] brotherly kindness love. [8]For if these things are yours and abound, they make you to be not idle nor unfruitful unto the knowledge of our Lord Jesus Christ. [9]For he that lacketh these things is blind, [g]seeing only what is near, having forgotten the cleansing from his old sins." (II Peter 1:3-9)

We do not want to forget that we have been cleansed from our sins. It is that knowledge that will keep us from sinning. So, it is necessary for us to seek the qualities that will transform us into Christ's image. Maturity is necessary. We should always be seeking the next step in our maturing process. Like Abraham who trusted God even with the life of his son, we must trust God with the promises He has given to us. We must be willing to sacrifice those promises to obey God's word.

"[12]Blessed is the man that endureth temptation; for when he hath been approved, he shall receive the crown of life, which the Lord promised to them that love him." (James 1:12)

It is not our own promises that we must seek. It is the will of the Father. It is not our own happiness or desires that we have to hold onto, it is trust in the Lord. And it is not our own abilities and plans that are needed to make it through circumstances, it is the Holy Spirit that guides us in all truth.

It is not an easy task to learn and live out the will of God. It is no easy task to stand in the faith through testing. It does not matter the test or the time it takes for the fulfillment of a promise from God. We must continue in faith.

The most difficult test I have had to endure was the trauma of a divorce. The pain of losing someone that I had spent more than a quarter of century with and had known for most of my life was most devastating.

The part of the marriage vows that states "for better or for worse", is easy enough to say but we never want or expect to experience the worse. We always want only the better. We think the worse is something that happens to someone else; maybe a spouse being ill or going through a rough spot. We do not think about it being someone who is hateful toward us or someone who walls us out of their lives. We do not think of the death and destruction of drugs or alcohol or adultery; or of lies, deceit or verbal distain that continues day after day, month after month or year after year. Worse can be the stress that weighs so heavy that you feel like you are being crushed under it. Or, it can be like the prophet, Hosea experienced with an unfaithful spouse. The whoring after others did not stop Hosea's love for his wife. It was painful for him, but his love continued.

I think that is what is often so hard for others to understand when we endure through faith. Others can see the pain and the wrong actions, but they do not see what God is doing. That mysterious bonding of spirit that only God can do is a force not seen by the human mind or eye. It is only experienced by the heart and soul. And the explosion that is experienced when man tries to pull it asunder is a shattering of the heart. It takes the fire of rage and hate to harden a heart so severely as to separate the love God uses to bond the spirits of a man and his wife. Unfortunately, like any bomb that explodes, the pieces that hit those around it can be devastating.

Whatever the test is, whether divorce, drugs, abuse, or many, many other circumstances, the response must be the same. The many thoughts and feelings experienced during testing are wide. Sadness, hurt, anger, confusion, doubt, love, fear, freedom, can all find their way through our soul. Even through all the emotions, the path we seek in the circumstance has to be God's will. Sadness and hurt want to isolate. Anger wants revenge but "vengeance is mine saith the Lord." Confusion throws circumstances in our face and invites doubt to ask what has happened to

God's promises. Love covers us and tells us that God has not forsaken us when fear threatens to steal confidence and freedom.

All the while as emotions surge and subside, it is important to remember that we live by faith and not by sight and that it is every word that proceeds from the mouth of God that is reality and not necessarily the circumstances that surround or even seem to engulf us. Our emotions will lie to us. They are not based in reality, but in perception. Like circumstances, they cannot be trusted. Our faith and our trust must be in Jesus.

We must know, trust, and follow God's word. If you do not know His promise for your life, seek Him. Spend time in prayer. If you are not sure what He is saying, read the Bible. If you need to feel His presence, praise and worship Him. It is our job to seek Him throughout our lives. And not just throughout our lives but through every moment. Yes, it takes more than a lifetime to know God, so we cannot waste a minute ignoring Him. God is always present, even in those silent times of testing.

So, what have we learned from God's testing? We learn just what Abraham learned. We must trust in God and in His promises. He is faithful.

Endless Struggle

Long and hard the years have been
The last three straight from hell
My struggle seems an endless one
And yet I know full well
Christ is my Redeemer
And to many I must tell
Of Love great and abiding
Of character strong and true
Of Christ my Lord and Savior
Who wants your love too!

Questions to Ponder

1. Are you patient or are you praying for patience?

   _____

   _____

2. Are you more concerned with what others say or what God says?

   _____

   _____

3. What are you willing or unwilling to sacrifice in your life?

   _____

   _____

4. Do you have expectations of what God will do?

   _____

   _____

5. When have you felt like God would not expect "that much" from you?

   _____

   _____

6. What are you unwilling to give up?

_____

_____

7. Do you allow your emotions to make decisions for you?

_____

_____

8. How much does society contribute to your beliefs?

_____

_____

9. What would be the hardest thing for you to let go of?

_____

_____

10. Can God's promises override your desires for the present?

_____

_____

CHAPTER SIX
"Not My Fault"

───

[12]*"Lord, have mercy on my son: for he is epileptic, and suffereth grievously; for oft-times he falleth into the fire, and oft-times into the water."* Matthew 17:15

We are always looking for someone to blame. We have a natural tendency to look for somewhere to place blame. There are many places where responsibility rests, however accepting responsibility for our actions is a difficult thing to do. We always want to place anything negative somewhere else. If it makes us feel better, you would think we would not mind taking the responsibility, but even then, sometimes we do.

We have an enemy and there are times it is his responsibility for troubles. In the instance of the man in this scripture, whose son was possessed by demons, he recognizes that the boy is not at fault. The self-inflicted hurt was not the boys own doing. Our enemy comes to steal, kill and destroy. Our own natural tendency is for preservation and not self-harm. So, the father rightly discerned where the responsibility rested here. Our own self-preservation tends to override self-harm.

Unfortunately, today, we are not willing to recognize that evil may be to blame for some of the things that happen in our lives. Recognizing evil's responsibility can be difficult. It can be especially difficult when we have been programed by society to dismiss the existence of evil. We are surrounded by movies, television and social media telling us that demons do not exist. How then do we place blame where nothing exists? That leaves us seeking someone else to blame. We have to first recognize that evil is real, and we must deal with it. Once we acknowledge that fact, our correctly assigning responsibility is made a little easier.

The thing that makes this so difficult to comprehend is the number of things we see around us that point to evil. People cutting themselves or hearing voices. This is not natural or normal. It is supernatural. It points to an evil in this world. But these are things to be discerned.

Discernment is important to us as Christians. Knowing whether to accept a responsibility or to reject it can be instrumental in whether we succeed or fail. Recognizing our faults and learning to correct them makes us stronger. However, admitting to something often makes us feel exposed or weak to the rest of the world. We recognize that the fault must be placed somewhere. Chance or fate are only words, until we come to a point where we do not know how to place responsibility. Then we do not mind wielding them to avoid feeling exposed or weak.

> [13] *"Each man's work shall be made manifest: for the day shall declare it, because it is revealed in fire; and the fire itself shall prove each man's work of what sort it is."* 1 Corinthians 3:13

The truth is like a spotlight. It will shine directly onto a problem and expose it. Even when we try to hide in darkness. The truth is something we do not often recognize in ourselves. It is seen by others. Our faults can shine brighter than anything else around us. We forget a testimony admitting guilt and correcting a problem is often seen by others as something commendable. To us, it feels like nakedness. Even things that we admire in others we tend of hide as best we can.

Others can see in us what we cannot see in ourselves. Sometimes we deceive ourselves more than we deceive others by our attempts to make ourselves look good. However, it will all eventually be exposed. Accepting and learning from the things we perceive as weaknesses can be strength for us.

"It's Not My Fault!" is a phrase we hear again and again in our society. Too often it is to cover or mask our own shortcomings. I can remember when my kids were little, hearing them and/or their friends whale "I didn't do it." They knew full well that they did. Furthermore, as mothers, my friends and I also knew they were responsible. Our protesting does not change the reality of a situation. Responsibility is something we do not wish to accept for ourselves.

A favorite thing, and often what seems easiest, is to blame our parents. Because we tend to replay our parents' words, whether encouragement or abusive, in our head, we pull them out first to blame. What they said or did or taught us, has to be the wrong thing for our current circumstance. Although scriptures tell us to "honor" our father and mother, we find it much easier to blame them.

When I was hundreds of miles away from home at college one weekend, I was invited by some friends to go on a ski trip. The reason I declined the invitation was because I had not asked my parents' permission to go. Who holds the responsibility for that? I had been raised by my parents to respect them and to ask permission for things. I failed to learn to think for myself. Who is responsible? The truth is, I am responsible. It did not matter if I was 18 or 30, my parents hold over me was a figment of my imaginations. If my parents still felt responsible for the outcomes in my life, they were being overprotective. If my parents ignored my coming and goings, it did not make them neglectful of my circumstances. When I reached an age where I was accountable for my own actions, they were no longer responsible for them.

Unfortunately, we see today, too great a blame placed on others. In James 3:5-6 it says *"So the tongue also is a little member, and boasteth great things. Behold, how much wood is kindled by how small a fire! And the tongue is a **fire**: the world of iniquity among our members is the tongue, which defileth the whole body, and setteth on **fire** the wheel of nature, and is set on **fire** by hell."* We wag our tongues so much to deflect fault from ourselves that we tend to hurt others. That is not likely our intent, but when we place blame on others, we can cause much more harm than good.

One of the ways we see this playing out today is in the many false accusations being alleged against people. Although our focus is often on the big name, it is something that is happening in all walks of life. Teenagers angry with a parent or a stepparent, allege sexual harassment to get revenge. They do not always understand that they are ruining a person's life with their words. Instead of accepting correction, they take what they perceive as the easy way out, blame someone else and deflect the problem to a different issue.

People are yelling racism, white supremacy, Nazi, fascist, anti-fascism and many more terms at one another. Definitions of words and consequences of how it affects others are being ignored. There is a whole lot of finger-pointing going on.

Again, and again we listen to testimonies and stories from others of how they endured circumstances and grew beyond them. We learn of struggles that people have gone through that only enriched their lives. We give them our honor, respect and encouragement because of their overcoming circumstances.

What we know is that there is more than one place where blame can be set. As Matthew 17:15 points out, it could be the fault of our enemy. For anyone that wishes to deny any spiritual or supernatural influence, it is easy to excuse or deny the presence of evil. However, man has an enemy. Remember that the enemy wants to appear as appealing as possible. Then it is important to acknowledge that he is a liar. When we recognize these two facts, we can better recognize when he is trying to misdirect blame to us.

We must also remember that we can be deceived. This is especially important for women. The feminist movement would immediately balk at such a statement, but it is backed up by scripture. Society must not dictate our beliefs. When we stand on God's word, we will often find ourselves in opposition to society. Trying to convince us that what society thinks and believes is right is one of the ways that the enemy attacks us through spiritual warfare. If we cannot be indoctrinated to believe what society says as truth, then the devil might try shaming us into believing it.

There is an unseen world around us that interacts with us and works to control us. To deny spiritual warfare is a mistake. When we see and understand how the enemy works to "steal, kill and destroy" us, we are better able to combat them by prayer and standing on the word of God. Denying the existence of the battle around us is like blindly walking through a war zone and smelling the roses in gardens that have not been destroyed.

Spiritual warfare is a large subject and deserves its own teaching. However, it is important that we never forget, it is real, and we are all influenced by it. Even Jesus Christ was hit with spiritual warfare when he was led to be tempted by the devil. First, he tried to steal Christ's faith. The devil dared Jesus to make the stones into bread because he had not eaten for 40 days. Secondly, the devil tried to kill him by getting him to throw himself from the highest point in Jerusalem. Lastly, the devil tried to destroy Christ's ministry by offering him the world. Jesus fell for none of these tricks. These ideas were easily justifiable. He was hungry, He knew what God had said about his safety and Jesus knew that Satan had the authority to grant Him rule over what He saw. But the truth was that Jesus was here for a much larger reason and He knew God and His plans. He knew what God's word said and He spent time in prayer with the Father. Jesus was able to see just how the devil was trying to deceive Him.

When you want to believe you are above being deceived, think of Jesus and how the enemy used tricks to try and deceive Him. The devil came to Jesus to steal, kill, and destroy Christ. He comes to us today to do the same thing. So, when something goes wrong, it may well be the responsibility of the devil. However, it may also be your own responsibility. I believe the closer we come each day to the return of Jesus Christ, the harder demons work to shame, blame and deceive us.

It does not matter how circumstances divert responsibility. When we feel exposed for our actions, we immediately want someone else to have responsibility. It is not always our own fault. There are times that the blame does rest on the shoulders of another person. Life is not fair and anyone that tells you it is, is working to deceive you.

Sometimes, others can cause our circumstances to work against us. The person who endures a murder of a loved one is not at fault. A spouse who married for life but is faced with an unwanted divorce is unjustly treated by life. Many circumstances in life will come along to crush us. It is then that it is important to remember Romans 8:28.

"And we know that to them that love God all things work together for good, even to them that are called according to his purpose."

No matter how hot it gets in any situation; no matter how exposed you feel; not matter how society tries to ridicule; it is always important to remember to stand on God's word.

ABANDONED

Alone is the feeling washing over my soul
Begging for pity to take hold
Asking the question "Why me?"
Never considering something better to unfold
Doubting every decision with no confidence around
Only wishing for a place to implode
Now wishing for a friendly embrace to
Envelope this heart that tries not to explode.
Doubts and loneliness make the abandoned heart cold.

QUESTIONS TO PONDER

1. What do you feel guilty about?

    _____

    _____

2. Do you ever find yourself wanting to place blame or responsibility on someone else?

    _____

    _____

3. Does accepting responsibility for your actions make you feel vulnerable or exposed?

    _____

    _____

4. Does accepting responsibility for your actions give you a feeling of empowerment?

    _____

    _____

5. Would you rather have someone telling you what to do?

_____

_____

6. If so, why? Do you feel you can give them all responsibility for how you react?

_____

_____

7. Do you have someone you can confide in to help you determine when you are responsible?

_____

_____

8. What is there in your life that you need to change to accept your own actions?

_____

_____

9. Do you have something that you need to accept responsibility for in your life?

_____

_____

10. What responsibilities have you neglected?

_____

_____

CHAPTER SEVEN
Stepping Outside God's Will

|||||||||||||||||||||||||||||||||||||||||||||||||||||||||||||||||||||||||||||||||||||||||||||||||||||||||||||||||||||||||||||||||

²¹ "As coals are to hot embers, and wood to fire, so is a contentious man to inflame strife. **Proverbs 26:21**

Coals burn long and hot. They affect all around them. Wood helps to keep a fire burning. This scripture compares just how insidious strife can be in our lives because of how other people affect us. It is a dangerous thing to step outside the will of God. So very often in our lives we hear the voice of our parents or others telling us who we associate with, will makes a big difference. If there are people that they believe to be a bad influence on us, we need to disassociate ourselves with them.

However, this never takes into consideration the feeling we have for those people. They can be people we have looked up to and admired. They might be a lifelong friend. They could be people that we have partnered with in different endeavors. Cutting those ties with different individuals can be more difficult than expected.

Sometimes, individuals' motives are evident. A drug dealer, whether a good friend or not, is not someone that we need to continue association with, in our lives. It is especially true if there is or has been a problem with drugs. Alcoholics, smokers, liars, adulterers, anyone with a negavie sway or influence on us, should be disassociated from us. Anyone that will influence us in a behavior that we want to stay away from. The temptation that their presence brings can be detrimental to us. The most difficult part of this disassociation is often that we do not recognize that if these people truly had our best interest at heart, they would want to distance themselves.

So, are we saying that evil has a greater influence on us than God? Not at all. We are saying, as people, we have limits and weaknesses. Our feelings toward others can complicate those tendencies. God expects us to follow Him and has told us that He will not temp us more than we can bear. However, if we place those temptations in our way, He does not remove them for us. He expects us to choose. We can choose the temptation, or we can choose God. Our own frailty does not always recognize that we have placed temptations, beyond our own abilities, in our way. We look to people, often of bad influence, to help us instead of looking to God for help.

God always has our best interest at heart. Individuals, especially those that burn with a desire to advance their own agenda, do not consider us first. Their influence in our life is that burning coal. And far too often we get burned.

Do not confuse the influence of others with temptation from God. These are two very different things. Any test[ii] we are presented with from the hand of God is for our own benefit. It will challenge us to be better. It will drive us to learn and study God's word. It will bring us closer to Him as we create a better relationship and bond with Him. The temptations we face from evil, through life and association with others are different. Temptation will draw us into sin. The scriptures tell us that the enemy comes to steal, kill and destroy us. Temptation outside of the hand of God does exactly that. It is designed to do everything possible to tear us down. It works to degrade our efforts.

Keeping our focus on God and what is good should always be our goal. It is not always without pain. There always comes a time in our lives where we must decide to remove someone from our lives that is detrimental to us. It is not difficult to walk away from someone that doesn't mean anything to us. Steeped in drug abuse, another user can mean nothing to us. However, the dealer that is always there to supply our addiction, is someone we come to think of as a friend. They are the person that "helps" us when we feel the worst. They encourage us, even if it is in a negative manner, so that we can feed the chains that bind us. They may be the very one who had been our good friend before introducing us to drugs. Removing that person will be painful for us.

The pain of removing someone from our lives can come, in a number of ways. The closer the relationship, the tighter our heart strings are tied to them. The pain of heartbreak is a pain we never want to feel. It is disturbing to us even when we see others endure it. Our concept of love can be clear, or it can be twisted. Either way, the pain felt from a broken relationship is painful.

Our disassociation with someone can be physically painful. In the case of an addiction, our physical bodies experience the negative affect of the withdrawal. Wither it is drugs, alcohol, smoking, eating or any other addiction, it can be a physically painful experience to change our habit(s).

The psychological changes we endure from severing a relationship can swing a wide berth. Depending on how someone has influenced our lives, the psychological effects can be easily endured or difficult. The words of a parent or sibling can blow through our heads throughout a lifetime. Whether they are uplifting or hurtful and debilitating, these psychological episodes can affect our behaviors. They can mean the difference in success or failure for us. Our dependence on what God has to say in any situation then becomes of utmost importance. The impact different individuals have on our lives can be just as influential to us.

We may even have to disassociate with someone on a spiritual level. If your views and beliefs are different and headed in different directions, there could have to be a disconnection from what appears to be a tight relationship. There can be many reasons for this disconnection. First there are different denominations in our society. The basic belief of salvation is fundamental. However, there can be subtle beliefs that one can strongly embrace while another totally disregards. If these can be worked through in a relationship, that is a wonderful thing. Sometimes, especially in a marriage, if both are not seeking God's answer, then the problem goes unresolved.

There are also times when other religions will clash. Buddhism, Hinduism, Muslim, etc. are not compatible with the Christian belief. We see over and over in scripture when people began to worship other gods because of the social influence they experienced. If we do not separate from a spiritual relationship, and the stronger personality from a differing religion influences our thinking, then we lose. Our focus must always be upon God.

There is also a political position that might have to be addressed. Although this might appear to be societal influence, or a political position, it is a struggle between good and evil. It is important that we always remain on the side of good and follow after Jesus for our answers and not the subtle nuisances' others want us to perceive.

There are a number of occasions in my life where I have heard individuals confess that the words of a teacher changed their lives. Any time we see someone with authority, we tend to place a higher expectation on their words than we might place on the words of anyone we consider an ordinary friend. Although we want to place our trust in God alone, the fact is that we are easily influenced by our culture to trust many that we do not know. For example, we might go to see a doctor or lawyer for advice. This could be someone we know, or someone recommended to us or even a stranger. We have placed that person in a position of authority over us and when given the advice we seek, we trust it. Our own belief system dictates our response. If a doctor tells you that you have cancer, it can immediately cause you fear. Whether it is true or false, whether he has taken all the necessary tests needed or not tends to fall by the way. If a lawyer tells you that your innocence in a crime does not matter, that it is less expensive and easier to accept a plea-bargain than to fight, your defenses are down, and acceptance can be its companion regardless of your truth.

So, we can see how we allow others to influence us, just simply by being within their vicinity. Our reality is that it can be painful for us to remove them from our lives. It can also be hurtful, if we allow them to continue to be an influence on us.

When you remove a coal from the embers around it, it begins to cool. The response is not immediate. Putting out the fire on a log does not mean it will not be singed or burned. There is always an effect. The amount of time we allow circumstances to affect us will determine the amount of damage done to us.

Years ago, I was faced with circumstances that I felt I could no longer endure. A nervous breakdown seemed so much more appealing to me. However, God graciously saved me from the long struggle of recovering from that. My turning to Him, instead of allowing circumstances to destroy me made a difference. It allowed me, my sense of integrity, and to not be ashamed of my past pain. It did not destroy the future influence I could have in encouraging people to trust in God. It gave me a testimony for faith and trust in our Lord that people can understand and relate to in their daily lives.

It is not always addiction that draws us into unholy relationships. Circumstances of life can change and twist where we find ourselves, without ever trying or expecting it, in circumstances that will change the direction of our lives. Take divorce for instance. When two people pledge their lives to one another in a loving relationship, they never expect to find themselves faced with a divorce. The incidental daily occurrences change them in a way never expected. They may become faced with temptations beyond their expectations. Or they can simply take different paths that lead them away from one another. Without concentrated effort to come together again, divorce can appear their only option.

An affair gives them the choice of walking away. They must walk away from the person that appears to fulfill their every delight or walk away from the one they have pledged to love through good times and bad; sickness and health. Non-commitment leaves a person with the choice to walk away. They can walk away from their indifference or walk away from their pledge of faithfulness.

Unexpected sickness or disability can face someone with a choice. They can face the trials that lay ahead, knowing the difficulties or they can walk away. A woman faced with an unwanted pregnancy today can be made to feel like her only choice is abortion. However, life is always a choice.

We must choose to live through the heartbreaks. We can trust God to take us through the physical and emotional pain we face in our lives. No matter how bruised our lives become because of the influences of others, we can recover. God can do amazing things with the lives of people who trust Him.

Although people and circumstances can influence our decisions, it is important that we remember to always look for what God is doing in our lives. We need to seek His purpose for our lives. He always has our best interest at heart. He will always use our circumstances for our benefit and His glory.

There will always be people to influence your life. Some will be good, and some will be bad. It is important that you recognize the difference. Those that have a good influence on you are relationships that you should cultivate to a higher degree. The people that encourage you to be the best you can be are ones that can help you to determine a greater success in your life. People who are willing to speak truth into your life and help you recognize your own weaknesses are important to have around.

These are people that will often anger you. We do not always want to see the worst of ourselves or to change. Human nature tells us that staying the same is best. However, we know that in life, things will change. We must change with them, or we become stagnant. An unwillingness to change can harden not only our hearts but personalities and character as well. Knowing the difference between what to change and what to keep can make a great difference in our outlook.

A Road Called Divorce

Tell me friend, you've been down this road
The one called divorce, before
Can you tell where the heartbreak ends
Is there a way to even the score?

    Take another road my friend,
    This isn't where you should go
    The trip is way too treacherous
    And the healing process slow.

But I was left without a choice
This road all I can take
My home and all the love I had
Was ripped and stomped to death.

    Be careful not to stumble,
    It's rocky up ahead
    There's grief, sadness and anger
    Each will walk with you my friend

Grief is looking for my soul,
It was ripped apart
And sadness is my companion
When loneliness comes each day

    Don't let them stay too long
    They will want to built a house
    But depression is a sandy foundation
    Keep moving –Watch those traps

Then give me some spite and I'll strike first
Put anger at the helm
I won't be defeated
Just wait, I'll show them!

    Anger's a bitter captain
    No partners does he have
    He only takes captives
    Of those whose reigns he has.

So how do I walk this road,
I don't know where it goes.
The only companions I have to take
Are enemies to my cause

    Keep looking up and watch the cross
    Follow it every step
    No matter the grief or sadness
    It will be your light

Is there any way around it.
I've heard this road is long
And no one else to walk with me
And my feelings tag along

    Carry hope upon your shoulders
    Put a smile upon your face
    Let the joy of the Lord surround you
    And you can't hurry the pace.

Thank you, friend for your advice
I'm more than a little scared
This isn't the road I'd hoped for
But you seem to have fared it well

    Remember too, to guard your heart,
    It first must mend
    Or love you try to fill it with
    Can too quickly end

The road ahead is a hard one
Remain faithful to the Lord
Watch out for all the pit falls
And you will stay the course.

    Jesus will go with you,
    He'll be there every step
    No matter how long it takes you,
    You'll reach forgiveness yet.

QUESTIONS TO PONDER

1. Have you had a time in your life where you knew there was someone influencing you that you needed to stay clear of the relationship?

   _____

   _____

2. Is there someone in your life today who holds a negative influence in your life?

   _____

   _____

3. Are their people that you should keep in your life but set boundaries with?

   _____

   _____

4. Is there someone you need to build a closer relationship with?

   _____

   _____

5. Who do you know that helps enrich your life and why?

_____

_____

6. What changes have you experienced that you know were beneficial?

_____

_____

7. Is there a change where you have experienced a great deal of pain?

_____

_____

8. Has anyone ever angered you, but you then had to admit they were right?

_____

_____

CHAPTER EIGHT
GOD REVEALS HIMSELF

IIIIIIIIIIIIIIIIIIIIIIIIIIIIIIIIIIIIIIIIIIIIIIIIIIIIIIIIIIIIIIIIIIIIIIIIIIIIIIIIIIIIIIIIIIIIIIIIIIIIIIIIII

"¹ Now Moses was keeping the flock of Jethro his father-in-law, the priest of Midian: and he led the flock to the back of the wilderness, and came to the mountain of God, unto Horeb. ² And the angel of Jehovah appeared unto him in a flame of fire out of the midst of a bush: and he looked, and, behold, the bush burned with fire, and the bush was not consumed. ³ And Moses said, I will turn aside now, and see this great sight, why the bush is not burnt. ⁴ And when Jehovah saw that he turned aside to see, God called unto him out of the midst of the bush, and said, Moses, Moses. And he said, Here am I. ⁵ And he said, Draw not nigh hither: put off thy shoes from off thy feet, for the place whereon thou standest is holy ground. ⁶ Moreover he said, I am the God of thy father, the God of Abraham, the God of Isaac, and the God of Jacob. And Moses hid his face; for he was afraid to look upon God. ⁷ And Jehovah said, I have surely seen the affliction of my people that are in Egypt, and have heard their cry by reason of their taskmasters; for I know their sorrows; ⁸ and I am come down to deliver them out of the hand of the Egyptians, and to bring them up out of that land unto a good land and a large, unto a land flowing with milk and honey; unto the place of the Canaanite, and the Hittite, and the Amorite, and the Perizzite, and the Hivite, and the Jebusite. ⁹ And now, behold, the cry of the children of Israel is come unto me:

moreover I have seen the oppression wherewith the Egyptians oppress them. [10] Come now therefore, and I will send thee unto Pharaoh, that thou mayest bring forth my people the children of Israel out of Egypt."
(Exodus 3:1-10)

This fire is particularly interesting. It is a fire that burns but does not consume. It is visible, warm and has a presence. It is in His grace and mercy that God reveals Himself to us. Just as Moses looked at a bush that was on fire, yet did not burn up, it is important that we look at our circumstances and see God's presence. Our circumstances can often show us God's infinite grace and mercy for us.

This scripture shows us how God revealed Himself and that He saw and heard the distress of His people. God had not left them. He was there and chose Moses for their deliverance. In the same way, God sees and hears us. We often forget, in the midst of circumstances, that He chooses others to help us.

THE FIRE

It was on a Saturday night. My son had been sitting at his desk working on a model car when a friend of his stopped by the house and told him that they had just seen his girlfriend's sister and a friend in a car wreck a few blocks away. They were not sure if his girlfriend was in the car or not. So immediately, both my sons and I jumped in the car to go and see if everything was alright. When we arrived, we found out that all three girls had been in the car and the sister had banged her knee but was not seriously hurt. Otherwise, everyone was OK.

So, we headed home. We all sat down to the dinner table to talk. My husband, at the time, was still on the computer in the back of the house. After a few minutes, my youngest son said that he smelled something, like it was burning. My older son had been burning a candle on his desk earlier, so we immediately went to his room.

Before even arriving at his door we knew there was trouble because smoke was pouring over the door frame. We looked in and the flames were about 12 to 18 inches high on the desk. By now, my husband is aware there is a problem. I went immediately to the telephone and called 911. My youngest son did as he was told and went outside. He was hesitant because he did not want to be alone right then. My oldest son stood frozen in astonishment at his door watching as his father surveyed the problem. We both told him to get out of the house.

I too went out the door with the children. My oldest son, so broken by the fire and feeling a great pain of guilt, wept as he leaned on our car. I let him know it was ok. We were glad that everyone was alright, and any damage would be taken care of.

Meanwhile, my husband worked at putting the fire out. He grabbed a large towel from the linen closet and soaked it in water and dumped it on the fire. His thinking was quick and effective. By the time the fire department arrived, the fire was out.

We realized just how fortunate we all were. With a built-in bookcase shelf immediately over the fire, In just the few minutes it took for the fire department to get there, we would have had a major fire if my husband's quick thinking and previous experience as a volunteer fireman had not kicked in to get the fire out.

However, the heavy black smoke was throughout the house. The firemen pulled a fan off the truck and began to pull the smoke out of the house. It only took a few minutes and then they were gone. As we came back into the house, we looked at the damage. A plastic cassette box, a cassette, model car parts and a plastic jewelry box were fused together on the desk. They were still hot, so we set them in a sink of water to cool. Two sketch pads were scorched, and several miscellaneous items burnt but overall, the loss was small.

We waited through the weekend to begin the process with the insurance company. By the time we had called them on Monday, we had thrown away the items that had burned, vacuumed up the ashes and begun to do enough to make things livable.

After calling the insurance company we found out that we would have to call a restoration company to come in and clean things up. As

I thought about it, I really wanted to do it myself to save the insurance money. If someone was going to be paid for cleaning my house, I wanted it to be me. On our agent's advice, we called restoration companies to come out and see what had to be done. The more we heard, the more I realized I could not do it all myself. There was more to be done than I knew how to do or was able to get done.

Many "if's," crossed my mind. **If** the fire had hit the model car paint; **if** it had hit the bookshelves over the desk; **if** the fire had happened on a weeknight when my husband was out of town; **if** any of us had been sleeping, etc. But God is faithful and there were no ifs. There was God's hand of protection on us all. And not just us, but on the things, He had given to us.

As a matter of fact, as I have reflected on it, I found only blessings in what is normally a tragedy. I believe that is because of God's great grace and favor. Because, if it were not for His great favor, there would be no if's. There would only be the tragedies, losses, and the emotional trauma to deal with in our lives. The hurt and pain would drown out everything else until such time that everything was put back together, and time could begin putting distance between us and the tragedy.

But because of God's wonderful grace and favor, we have many great blessings. What we had was very little loss, a restoration company that came in and cleaned everything, and a painter to repaint the house. Every carpet cleaned and every tile floor cleaned and waxed. The entire house cleaned and painted. The furniture cleaned and polished. With all these things being done, we could have sat back and done nothing. We chose to pitch in and help because we wanted to see it done, and also to save some money.

SEEING GOD

Just as God revealed himself to Moses in a burning bush and just as He revealed Himself to me through a small house fire, He will reveal Himself to you in your life. The wonderful thing is we do not have to wait for an external fire. God has placed the fire of passion in our hearts and in our hands through His Holy word, the Bible.

It would be nice if God would set a bush on fire and talk to us through it. We could just walk out our door and ask God what He wanted for us that day. But God is neither our puppet master nor our personal concierge. God placed a brain between our ears and expects for us to use it. Besides, too many of us would probably argue either with ourselves; wondering if it were really God or with God Himself.

We are privileged today to have the written word. The Bible was not something Moses had on his bedside table. As a matter of fact, he was not even able to head down to the local temple to hear scripture read for encouragement and instruction. Moses was dependent upon hearing directly from God. Moses lived in a day before the construction of the temple in a land where many gods were worshipped.

We too can hear directly from God. Chances are that you are never going to hear an audible voice telling you what to do. I will not say that will not or cannot happen because God can do whatever He deems necessary. Most likely, you will hear His still small voice tugging at your heart or mind. You will recall a passage of scripture you heard someone speak or that you read. Like Moses you might wonder what that was and seek further to determine the origin behind it.

It is always a good thing to further seek what you do not understand. That is true in education, science, politics, or any aspect of life. It is especially true with God. He wants to reveal Himself to us. He wants us to know Him better. For it is in knowing Him better that we understand Him. Forming a closer relationship is what God is always about. He knows us and He wants us to know Him.

It is fascinating to know that the Creator of the universe, the one that breathed life into us, the one who knows even the number of hairs on our head, is the same one that desires for us to know Him. God seeks for us to understand His character and nature. He has given us scripture to make that easier for us.

I believe the study and history of the scriptures is very interesting. Books have been written and many theories and debates have gone on about who wrote what and how a final version came together. Two things give us proof of God and show us how important He feels His word is to us:

1. The Bible was written by many, over thousands of years, and is congruent and relevant
2. Although many have tried to destroy it, it has survived;

He intends for us to see Him. We can see God in more than just the Scriptures. God is also revealed in nature. The beauty of God's creation is all around us. The beautiful hues of a sunrise or sunset show the glory of God. The intricate details of something as simple as a leaf show us how deeply he cares. The precious face of a newborn child or the smile on a face reveals God's love, not only in our sight, but to our hearts. The warmth of God's love can be seen as well as felt through others.

And let us not forget that although God revealed Himself to Moses through the burning bush, He did not light up shrubbery all over Egypt. He revealed Himself to the Israelites through their deliverance. It was Moses who told them and led them. It was circumstances that showed them God. So, we cannot discount the fact that people and circumstances are part of the toolbox God uses to reveal Himself.

Sometimes, we have to look a little closer to see. If we focus only on the circumstance or on some outrageous thing that someone says, we could miss out. We do not all see things the same way and when we believe we are "right" or "know" what is going on and close our hearts and minds to the possibility that God is doing something, we could miss the blessings He has in store for us.

Once God revealed to Moses that He was going to use Him to lead the Israelites out of Egypt, where they were enslaved, a lot had to happen. There were plagues and loss of life. None of these things made it any easier on the slaves. They had to endure through these things too. Image for a minute with me, how some of the slaves in Egypt felt when all they saw were the plagues, destruction, and harsher treatment. Do you think they were telling themselves "Yeppee! God is at work!"? I am thinking, like us, they were complaining. I am sure that more than one Israelite slave lashed out at Moses or their family because of the circumstances. How many do you think asked their captors to hide them or keep them from this mad man?

It is amazing to me the lengths that God will go to for us to see Him. Not only did He arrange it so His people, who were slaves, would be released but the Egyptians also gave them gold and other possessions to leave. Then, God, in the midst of grumbling and complaining, delivered them from their enemy by parting the Red Sea. But He did not stop there. He also defeated the attacking enemy in the Red Sea so that they could not pursue His people further.

God used miracle after miracle to show Himself to His people. But, instead of rejoicing and embracing who God is, they continued to ignore Him. As a result of their disobedience, they wandered in the desert for forty years. A journey of that magnitude is going to take time. There were over a million people in this passage from Egypt to Israel. At most it should have taken months. Instead, it was a generation because they refused to embrace God. Some never saw the Promised Land. Some finally saw it, but never got there.

We are just like the slaves that hid or ignored what was going on. We can miss the forest for the trees. We can be more willing to hold onto our own image and comfort than to acknowledge God in our circumstances. Instead of receiving the blessings that God has planned and set aside for us, we grumble and complain, ignore and deny and eventually delay or destroy our chances for God's blessings for us. It is always so astonishing to me that God is in each circumstance. We do not always see it, but His saving grace is forever present. No matter the circumstance, God is still in control.

I often must remind myself of that fact because circumstances can draw me away from the truth. It is important to remember the old saying, that hindsight is 20/20. It takes us standing on faith, to know God's will. His Word and promises are where we find joy and/or contentment in whatever the circumstances are surrounding us.

Remember to look for God in the midst of the circumstances and trust what He is doing. He is still delivering His people today.

Basking In The Sunset

Basking in the sunset
Of heavens brilliant hues
Reflecting on the daily grind
And thinking Lord of you.

So little I've accomplished
Just what was today worth?
Would you be pleased with what I've done
This day upon your earth?

Did my life have meaning?
Was your purpose fulfilled?
Or did I wander within myself
Just looking for selfish thrills?

Remind me when the sun comes up
That the glory that I see
Is all your reflection
And to stay upon my knees

I will seek you in the morning
And through each and every day
That when my final sunset comes
I'll be with you always.

Questions to Ponder

1. Can you look at your life and see the hand of God through circumstances that seemed to be destructive or difficult?

_____

_____

2. Can you recognize how God has delivered you from something that would be far worse than just wondering around in His presence?

_____

_____

3. Have you complained long and hard about something that ended up being to your benefit or allowed you a freedom you would never have known otherwise?

_____

_____

4. What blessings do you see in looking back on your circumstances?

_____

_____

5. Do you feel you have been delayed in receiving any blessings?

_____

_____

6. Have you missed out on any blessings because of disobedience?

_____

_____

7. What circumstances around you show you God?

_____

_____

8. What blessings can you find in tragedy?

_____

_____

9. Can you lead someone to see a blessing even through their grumbling?

_____

_____

CHAPTER NINE
EXPECTATIONS

|||||||||||||||||||||||||||||||||||||||||||||||||||||||||||||||||||||||||||||||||||||||||||||||||||||||||||||||||||||||||||||||||||||||||

15"...Yea, four that say not, Enough: 16 Sheol; and the barren womb; The earth that is not satisfied with water; And the fire that saith not, Enough. 17 The eye that mocketh at his father, And despiseth to obey his mother, ..." Proverbs 30:15b-17a

We live our lives with expectations. Even as children, our parents have expectations for us. Others also expect children to behave in a certain way and parents to discipline in a certain way. Children have expectations of their parents. Boss' have expectations of employees. Churches have expectations for pastors and other members. Non-Christians have expectations of Christians. Friends have expectations for one another. Siblings have expectations. There is always someone expecting something. However, we can never live up to others' expectations. We have enough trouble living up to our own expectations.

God too, has expectations for us. He has a standard for our living and expects us to follow the rules. The difference in His expectations and those of others is two-fold. First, He lets us know what His expectations are. His expectations are high, and He knows that we are unable to meet those expectations on a continual basis. Thus, the second part of His provisions. Because he understands that His creations are imperfect, He made exceptions for His expectations. He gave Jesus Christ for our redemption when those expectations are not met.

That begs the inevitable question; So, can we continue sinning? This is a question that has already been raised and answered in Romans.

1 What shall we say then? Shall we continue in sin, that grace may abound? 2 God forbid. We who died to sin, how shall we any longer live therein? (Romans 6:1-2)

God has already addressed our questions. He has placed His expectations in scripture that we can learn and obey them. Although we may not reach perfection, we are able to read and study to know what God's expectations are for us.

Meeting the expectations of others is far harder to achieve, especially for Christians. Those who take a position against God expect their own version of perfection from Christians. Although few have ever studied what God says or expects, they believe they innately know. Their expectations are filtered through their own learning, morals and experiences. Whereas one person may believe that adultery is wrong for a Christian, another may believe that homosexuality should never be condemned by a Christian. Both believe the other is wrong and expects the Christian to embrace their thinking. These two issues are different sides to the same coin. Both are condemned in scripture but hold different expectations from different people.

Whereas many people expect perfection at the point of salvation, God sees the beginning of a process. Because we all start at different points in time and in our lives, God expects us to start where we begin. He does not expect an end result when we accept Jesus. He expects us to be a new creation and grow from where we begin. God does not expect perfection from the beginning.

People can often change their opinions of us and God when they see the unexpected. They can expect God's vengeance when they see what happens to a Christian. However, when they witness His grace instead, it can transform their thinking. In Acts 28 when Paul was bitten by a venomous snake in scripture, the outcome was not what the barbarians expected. Instead, they saw God's grace. They changed their minds.

It is important that we live according to God's expectations and not according to mans. When we try to live up to the expectations of others, we will always bring disappointment. Some will be happy while others will be greatly disappointed. This is due to the difference in the filters that everyone has for their lives and for others.

Our own expectations can also be a great disappointment. It is important to remember that we have our own filters and experiences that are not in line with those of God. I knew a woman once that because of the importance that bowling had taken in her life, she realized that she had made an idol out of it and it had therefore become sin to her. Few would ever think of bowling as sinful. This is a great example of how we can bring something that is common and generally considered innocent into a position of corruption for us. Anything in our lives that we place above Christ and make into an idol, becomes sin.

Stepping away from such sin can be difficult. It can be especially difficult if those around us think of our revelation as silly. We can be convinced that we are "blowing things out of proportion". The expectation of our sin from others does not have to hold the same weight as the expectation of God. When God reveals something to us through His scripture or through prayer, it is our job to be obedient to Him and not to the expectations of others.

When my friend explained that she could not participate in bowling with the rest of us, she did not do it because of our view of the circumstances. She did it out of obedience to God. God commands "Thou shalt have no other gods before me" (Exodus 20:3). Her obedience was to that command from God and not the ideas of her friends.

The truth of scripture will never stop the expectations of others. Those will always live on. But the truth of scripture should cause us to pause when we begin projecting our expectations onto others. Our concerns should always be for the best. We need to direct our expectations toward making our own actions more acceptable.

Our expectations of others can be construed as judgment. No one likes to be judged. We do not like to be told we are wrong in anything. We do not even like to be told when or how to do something. I think it is important here to remember that we are never told not to judge, but we are told that we will be judged in the same way that we judge. When we place our expectations on someone and judge them for that, then we will be judged by a strict rule of expectations.

God's word gives us guidelines. It also tells us that as disciples of Christ we are to encourage and teach others. It is not wrong to encourage others to follow those guidelines. However, they may not know or understand them in the same way that you understand them. Because we have the ten commandments, many people know and understand the basics of these rules. Some make a harsher judgment for some than others.

We find the ten commandments in Exodus chapter 20. Let's look at our sixth commandment. Because the King James version of scripture, as does the American Standard which we quote in this book, uses the word kill. It is a word that many grew up with and have embraced. However, many translations, including some of the more modern, like the Living Bible and the Message, use what I believe to be a more accurate word, murder. Verse 13 says we should not murder!

This commandment shows us the importance of life. God places a high value on people as evidenced in this command. We must not murder. However, when Jesus came, he expanded our understanding of Exodus 20:13. In Matthew 5 He explains that to murder someone is more than just taking life from their body. It is an attitude of the heart. So, when we degrade someone our sin of murder is as great as the one who separates a soul from the body. God's expectation is much higher than ours.

Having such an expectation for us to live by, God still made provision for our forgiveness and His grace. He allows us to grow in every area of our lives into His expectations. If you smoke, drink, curse, do drugs and have a multitude of things that are idols in your life when you come to know Christ, he does not expect instant perfection. He may begin to work on your addiction to drugs while allowing you to continue to cuss and drink. He may remove all sinful desires from you at once. God looks at who you are and gives you grace according to His expectations of you, not the expectations of others.

"Can a man take fire in his bosom, And his clothes not be burned?" Proverbs 6:27

To place you in relationships with other believers, it may be important to have another believer that helps you as you learn God's word. You may feel judged. You may have that burning feeling in your chest while all along, it is the Holy Spirit using someone in your life. They may be trying to help you understand what God means. I have found in life, that we often feel the presence of God's Holy Spirit convicting us through the words of others. Getting past hurt feelings to truth can be an obstacle. But it is an obstacle worth overcoming.

If you allow your feelings to dictate your life, rather than truth, you will find a hard road. It is important to remember that although our feelings are important, they can mislead us. If someone tells you that you can commit murder when you slander someone, you may have hurt feelings and be angry. However, the truth is what Jesus taught and not your feelings.

Meeting our own expectations is hard. We have a tendency to make our expectations too high or too low. We can continually disappoint ourselves by setting our expectations higher than we can obtain. Then we disappoint ourselves. The other end of the spectrum is that we set our standards too low, leaving us with the feeling of never accomplishing anything. In both of these scenarios, we allow our feelings to dictate where we are headed and our final reactions.

When we allow God to set the standard, and depend upon Him to get us there, disappointment is not the outcome. I am not saying that it is always easy because God will challenge us. However, when we look to Him for our answers, we can accept who we are and the outcome of what we accomplish.

> *"Set me as a seal upon thy heart, As a seal upon thine arm: For love is strong as death; Jealousy is cruel as Sheol; The flashes thereof are flashes of fire, A very flame of Jehovah."* Song of Solomon 8:6

It is God's great love that gives us grace while we learn what His word means in our lives. It is His expectations that we must meet. When we follow after His expectations, our life is far less stressful than if we try to meet the expectations of others or even of ourselves.

When we set goals in accordance with God's expectations, there comes a time when we realize that we have met that goal and have surpassed it. You can one day look back and say, "I use to..." You may have a date where you achieved your goal. You may know exactly when you overcame a particular problem. But it can be surprising when you one day look back to see that the problem no longer exists for you.

Overcoming a problem may put you in a position to help others. There are many drug addicts that now council others through their addictions. When you lose weight, stop smoking or accomplish any number of issues that can be overcome, there is always someone that wants to know how you did it. You become the example instead of having the expectation.

It is important that we remember that our lives are to be lived by the expectations of God and the example of Christ. We do not and never will live up to the expectations of others. Those change from person to person. God's expectations stay the same from generation to generation. So, let the "flashes of fire" be that of our Jehovah (God).

Words of the Spirit

Lord you pour from my mouth words of lessons learned
Speaking healing and truth to hearts broken & torn
Your words from the scriptures spill forth like a flood
Words safely hidden til needed; not forgotten but unturned

Turned up to grow faith in new Christians and old
Words needed to encourage, give hope and make bold
So, hide in my heart Your sweet words of truth
That in prayer and in wisdom I can speak them for you

For healing of hearts and bodies and minds
For bring new hope for people of all kinds
For imparting the faith you have given so freely
And anointing those called going out where you lead

Speak to my mind my soul and my heart
Wisdom for life you wish to impart
Give me opportunity and means to speak for you
So people with will, abundant life is for more than a few

QUESTIONS TO PONDER

1. Whose expectations are you trying to follow?

    _____

    _____

2. How have you succeeded or failed in following expectations?

    _____

    _____

3. Why is knowing God's word important to follow expectations?

    _____

    _____

4. Do you need to change your perspective on where you are headed?

    _____

    _____

5. How does God's word differ from what you are trying to accomplish?

    _____

    _____

6. Will meeting the expectations you place on yourself make you happy?

_____

_____

7. How can you fulfill God's expectations for you?

_____

_____

8. Have your expectations of others prevented you from affording grace?

_____

_____

9. How can you change your expectations of yourself and/or of others?

_____

_____

CHAPTER TEN
PREPARATION AND PROTECTION

||||||||||||||||||||||||||||||||||||||||||||||||||||||||||||||||||||||||||||||||||||||||||||||||||||||||||||||||||||||||||

"12 And Jehovah spake unto Moses and Aaron in the land of Egypt, saying, ² This month shall be unto you the beginning of months: it shall be the first month of the year to you. ³ Speak ye unto all the congregation of Israel, saying, In the tenth day of this month they shall take to them every man a [a]lamb, according to their fathers' houses, a lamb for a household: ⁴ and if the household be too little for a lamb, then shall he and his neighbor next unto his house take one according to the number of the souls; according to every man's eating ye shall make your count for the lamb. ⁵ Your lamb shall be without blemish, a male a year old: ye shall take it from the sheep, or from the goats: ⁶ and ye shall keep it until the fourteenth day of the same month; and the whole assembly of the congregation of Israel shall kill it [b]at even. ⁷ And they shall take of the blood, and put it on the two side-posts and on the lintel, upon the houses wherein they shall eat it. ⁸ And they shall eat the flesh in that night, roast with fire, and unleavened bread; with bitter herbs they shall eat it. ⁹ Eat not of it raw, nor boiled at all with water, but roast with fire; its head with its legs and with the inwards thereof. ¹⁰ And ye shall let nothing of it remain until the morning; but that which remaineth of it until the morning ye shall burn with fire. ¹¹ And thus shall ye eat it: with your loins girded, your shoes on your feet, and your staff in your hand; and ye shall eat it in haste: it is

Jehovah's passover. [12] For I will go through the land of Egypt in that night, and will smite all the first-born in the land of Egypt, both man and beast; and against all the gods of Egypt I will execute judgments: I am Jehovah. [13] And the blood shall be to you for a token upon the houses where ye are: and when I see the blood, I will pass over you, and there shall no plague be upon you [c] to destroy you, when I smite the land of Egypt." (Exodus 12:1-13)

This fire gives us a beautiful example of God's care over us. Knowing the story helps us in this instance. The fire here is used to prepare a meal. This meal must be prepared in a specific manner. God gives instruction for how the lamb or goat is to be cooked; but more than that, He gives them instructions of what to do in preparing to cook and what will happen.

This Passover took place while the Israelites were still captive in Egypt. God had already bombarded the land with a series of plagues to persuade Pharaoh to free the Israelites to return to their homeland. As God prepared to allow death to every firstborn child, He also prepared safety for His people. His provision was to protect them from danger and prepare them to leave.

If God's instructions were not followed, destruction and death would follow. One of the things that God wants from His people is obedience. That is true for us today. When we see and believe the purpose and plan God has for us, it makes obedience simple. During this scriptural instance, obedience was a life and death issue. It can be so for us today. In our world today, we do not always take time to see God's plan, only the inconvenience. We also tend to rationalize away His plans instead of choosing to believe in them.

In the same way, I do not believe following God's plan was easy or convenient for the Israelites at the time. This was a community of slaves. Freedom was foreign to their thinking. Someone else had always been responsible for their lives, and for generations, they simply did what they were told.

Plus, like the Egyptians, they had already endured a number of plagues. Each plague focused on one of the gods worshiped by the Egyptians. First was Sobek who Egyptians believed was the god of the waters. As such, he was often identified with the sun god Ra. The first plague endured as that of God turning the waters of the Nile into blood. The Nile was the life water of Egypt. Turning it to blood would have caused not only thirst for the people but a collapse in the harvest. Crops would not have been watered.

I want to add a note here. God is a God of order and as we progress through the plagues and how the Egyptian god had no power, you will see God's order building upon itself.

Secondly, came the frogs. Heket was a goddess of fertility and had the head of a frog. Because the magicians in Egypt were able to copy many of the miracles produced, Moses was asked to kill the frogs. This was done, thus showing the goddess of fertility was struck down.

Next came gnats or lice that were created from the dust of the earth. This Egyptian god was Ged. Lice plagued both men and animals. Even the magicians, unable to reproduce this miracle said that was part of the finger of God.

The Egyptian god of creation, Khepri, had the head of a fly. He too was associated with Ra. Khepri was considered the morning sun and a subordinate of Ra.

Next came Hathor, a goddess with the head of a cow. The plague that brought the death of livestock would have caused a great economic impact on the country. Not only would they have been hit with problems with crops but also with transportation, farming, food, military supplies and anything produced from the livestock.

The sixth plague that hit the Egyptian people while Moses ask for the freedom of the slaves was that of boils. Isis was worshiped as the goddess of medicine and wisdom. Both the mother of life and the crone of death, being unable to soothe the ills of her people would have been a great embarrassment.

When hail rained down from the sky, not only did it destroy the crops, it would have been an embarrassment for the goddess Nut, goddess of the sky.

The god, Seth, was the Egyptian god of storms. It was the eighth plague God used to finish the destruction of any crops that would have been left after the hail.

Ra was an important god to the Egyptians. He not only represented light but also growth and warmth. As such an important god, blackening the sun would have denied his power.

As we have seen with these nine plagues on Egypt, they are increasing menacing and destructive. Each would have been an endurance for everyone. But it is the tenth and final plague that brings the country to its knees and frees the Israeli slaves. This tenth plague was a direct attack on the Pharaoh himself, considered to be a god.

The Jewish people had endured weeks under stressful circumstances, and now God wanted a meal prepared and consumed as instructed. God was showing them that the gods they had known were not powerful, but the One True God was powerful. Also, that He saw their plight.

I cannot imagine the stench from the slaughtered animals at twilight and the blood spread around the doors was very appetizing. But they had lived with the stench of several plagues over the previous weeks. I believe these trials had boosted their faith level and they were beginning to understand God's faithfulness and that He was making a way for their freedom. So, they prepared for their meal.

Then, they waited. I am sure the waiting was the most difficult part of the night. I would imagine that not many of them slept. Even today, when we are anxious, we lose sleep. They would be listening for what would happen. They listened to the cries in the night, cries of grief and sadness. There was also anticipation. How many of their friends were disobedient and lost family? Already they had seen how Pharaoh had defied God and stood firmly against the Israelites release. Pharaoh's heart hardened with each defiant act. Would Pharaoh now take this great loss across the land out on them, or would he set them free? Would Pharaoh finally give in and acknowledge that he was only a man and that there was a God? Would the Israelites be leaving the only homes they had known for a foreign land filled with milk and honey?

There is a fine line between anticipation and worry. I believe both played a part in the hearts of the Jewish people. The same can be said of us today. While one person will hear God's word and anticipate something great and wonderful, another will worry about what will happen. It is important that we prepare for what God has ahead. Since we know He has a plan, we must also believe that whether we see good or bad for ourselves, it is God's plan being working out through our lives. Christ came so we could have an abundant life. We need not worry. Instead, we should look at the future and stir up anticipation.

Once God prepared His people, he protected them. For everyone who had prepared as God instructed, their firstborn was spared from death. The salvation provided was not solely dependent upon God's provision. It was also dependent on acceptance of God's word and obedience. The spirit of death that swept through the night was very real and very specific. Death came to claim the firstborn. Not just the first child in each household, but the firstborn of both man and beast. I imagine this was so that every household would be affected. Logic tells us there would be households without a firstborn child. Both husband and wife could be other than a first born with no children, thus exempting them from the coming event. However, if firstborn animals were also affected, it is logical that no household would be spared. It was important that every household be touched by God's judgment. He wanted everyone to know that it was by His hand they were delivered.

Finally, we have God's provision. After the preparation and protection that He provided, God also gave His people provision. They were not to leave Egypt empty handed. How could they make such a long journey without provision? They were slaves! What could they possibly have to start a new life? We see in Exodus 12: 31-36 just how well God provided for them.

> *"³¹ And he called for Moses and Aaron by night, and said, Rise up, get you forth from among my people,*

both ye and the children of Israel; and go, serve Jehovah, as ye have said. [32] Take both your flocks and your herds, as ye have said, and be gone; and bless me also. [33] And the Egyptians were urgent upon the people, to send them out of the land in haste; for they said, We are all dead men. [34] And the people took their dough before it was leavened, their kneading-troughs being bound up in their clothes upon their shoulders. [35] And the children of Israel did according to the word of Moses; and they asked of the Egyptians jewels of silver, and jewels of gold, and raiment: [36] and Jehovah gave the people favor in the sight of the Egyptians, so that they let them have what they asked. And they despoiled the Egyptians."

The Egyptian people came to recognize that it was by the one and only true God's hand, because of His enslaved people, that He had sent the plagues. They were ready for the Israelites to leave quickly. Therefore, the Egyptians gave them the provisions to go. They gave the Israelites cattle, gold, silver and even dough that was rising before it was baked. When the Jews left Egypt, they left with riches.

These people who had been slaves were now accepting control. They were no longer victims but are now people moving into a position of responsibility. The Israelites were not familiar with this new way of life and found it necessary to depend on God's guidance. Just as we struggle today with new concepts, so did these Israelites. Because of everything God had taken them through, they could have the confidence that He would provide for the future. This took a new way of thinking and was not an easy concept.

I think if you had told them that they would spend the next forty years wandering in the desert, they would not have left their homes. The change would have been too much for them to comprehend. I believe their doubts would have far outweighed their faith for such an extended time. Today, God does not tell us everything He is doing. We must learn to deal with the struggles as they come our way. The faith we have today is not the same faith that will carry us through the future. Faith must grow and mature. In some it will have to endure trials while others will need renewed faith so, in wavering it is not lost.

Let us revisit our look at the fire used in the preparation for this community. Remember that as they prepared for their Passover meal, the meat was to be roasted? Roasting is a slow process where heat penetrates. The hotter the fire, the faster the roast and the quicker the meal is ready. But this takes skill. If the fire is too hot, you will burn what you're cooking. Too cool, and it will take a long time before it is ready. Similarly, God knew what it would take to prepare the Egyptians to release their Jewish slaves and what it would take for His people to want to leave their homes. He dealt with both the stubbornness of the Egyptian Pharaoh and people and the doubts and fears of the Jewish slaves.

Also, God instructed the Israelites to burn up whatever meat was left over. God did not provide for any leftovers. Similarly, God does not want us to revisit what is past. That can be very difficult to do. Once the Jewish people were in the desert and had a little time to think, they were ready to return to the familiar. They had been surrounded, their entire lives, by idols. They only knew of someone else being responsible for their well-being and care. While Moses was on the mountain, they became restless and needed direction. Instead of seeking God, their slave mentality set in and they expected a man to tell them what to do. They wanted to avoid the pressure of change and the responsibility they increasingly felt.

We make these same mistakes. When God prepares us for His plan, protects and provides for us, we still do not want change to happen. We want what we want, when and how we want or expect it. We become impatient. We try and go back, seeking what is familiar. But God has burnt up the past. It will never be palatable again. What He has ahead is far better than we can imagine.

So, no matter the doubts, anxiety or time needed to press forward, it is important for us to remember that what is ahead is much grander and more promising than what we have left behind. We also need to pay attention to the provisions we have. They are greater than what we left behind. Most importantly, we need to seek God instead of what is familiar to us. Immersing ourselves in food, alcohol, drugs, sex or any other distraction will never give us the direction we need to move forward into God's promises. It is only when we follow Him that we will make it to the promises He has set before us.

Guard My Heart

How do you guard your heart from the things of this world
From the majesty of the mountains and the breezes of the sea
From the birds and squirrel and wildlife caught in play
Or from the painted sunset that slips below the bay

How do you guard your heart from the people in this world
From smiles and laughs and the children's pouts and frowns
From those that have only your best interest at heart
Or from those tears you see pouring when someone falls apart

How do you hide your heart from the passion of this world
From ears that hear the soft sweet sound of every spoken word
From eyes that gaze across a room and cannot break the stare
Or from the heart of newborn love whose spark begins to flare

Teach me Lord to guard my heart while I am in this world
Guard it from the hardness that creeps in with harsh words
Guard it from the sadness of loosing those so dear
Or from the deep despair when loved ones cannot be near

Teach me Lord to guard my heart while I am in this world
From selfishness that steals away the passion of your love
From hurt that distracts me from the joy in knowing you
And from sins enticement disguised in royal hues.

Keep me Lord and guard my heart while I am in this world
Help me Lord to love whether friend or enemy appears
Help my life to reflect your passion that love may abound
And take me home when I am done with a heart you have crowned

QUESTIONS TO PONDER

1. What event in your life has God delivered you from?

   _____

   _____

2. How has God made things uncomfortable for you in the past?

   _____

   _____

3. Is there someone that holds you in slavery?

   _____

   _____

4. Who or what has God protected you from?

   _____

   _____

5. What events have brought you to the conclusion that God was not listening?

   _____

   _____

6. What preparations did you have to make to fulfill God's promises?

_____

_____

7. How have your own perceptions differed from God's plans for your life?

_____

_____

8. Have you done anything that would postpone or prevent you from enjoying God's benefits?

_____

_____

9. What struggle have you discovered to be a blessing, or miracle in your life?

_____

_____

CHAPTER ELEVEN
COMMITMENT

||||||||||||||||||||||||||||||||||||||||||||||||||||||||||||||||||||||||||||||||||||||||||||||||||||||||||||||||||||||||||||||||||||||||||||||||||||||||||||||

"And Peter had followed him afar off, even within, into the court of the high priest; and he was sitting with the officers and warming himself in the light of the fire." Mark 14:54

It seems that we have made "commitment" a dirty word today. It is actually a term of endearment. Whether you are committing to a person or something you wish to accomplish, it takes commitment. Olympians do not get to compete on that world stage without being committed to their training. To accomplish anything, it is important to make a commitment to follow through.

When we decide to follow Christ, it takes commitment. We must first commit our souls to the care of Jesus Christ. We must then commit to follow His teachings. If we want to become like Him, we must commit to making Him the Lord of our life.

The challenges we face in life are not easily overcome. The reality of life is that we will have challenges. If we commit our lives to Jesus Christ, we step into a role of building a relationship. That alone could be a foreign concept to some. Some may not even know how to build a relationship. Isolation may feel more comfortable.

Isolation, however, is a dangerous step for us to take. When we place ourselves out of the reach of others and isolate ourselves, we are removing ourselves from help. It is often an easy thing to do. It does not always feel like that is what we are doing until the loneliness sets in. When we are unable to step up and ask for help, we know that we have isolated ourselves.

This condition can happen out of pride. Many times, we learn to depend upon ourselves. We hear the old phrase "If you want something done right, you have to do it yourself!" There are times in life where we must do things ourselves. However, it is always better when there is someone alongside to cheer you on or to share your accomplishment. Isolation prevents us from sharing those moments. It can slip in under our radar if we are not willing to commit.

The circumstances of ignorance, isolation, or pride should not be factored into our thinking. As with anything in life, commitment takes practice. A couple starting a new marriage has committed themselves for a lifetime. That does not mean they totally understand what they are getting into at the time. When making a commitment, we do not necessarily see all the hills and valleys we must navigate. The fairy tale love that says "I do" is not the same love that holds a hand fifty years later. The struggles that happen from day to day can put a great strain on that commitment but, it is in remembering that commitment that will keep you going.

The sore muscles experienced during training for the Olympics is not what pushes an athlete forward to win a gold, silver, or bonze metal. It is the commitment they make and the passion they have to be the best that sets them on the winners stand.

Anything worth accomplishing in life, is worth the commitment. But pushing aside a commitment to follow your own path will not achieve the joy you receive from sticking with a commitment when things get hard. I am reminded of Yoda when he said "Try not. Do or do not do." We can try many things, but it is not until we decide to commit that we come to a point to do what we want to accomplish.

Commitment is not the dirty word that many in society have made it out to be. Those who want to lower standards rather than to raise them are the ones that make commitment into a dirty word. A non-committal attitude is enjoyed by those who want to take the easy road.

When we commit our lives to Christ, we are making a lifetime commitment. There will be many things during your life that will come along to sidetrack that commitment. People will disappoint you in their walk with Jesus. Churches will hurt you because you will have greater expectations for members than they are able to reach. Or maybe, they don't even know or understand your expectations. Life will throw you curve balls to make it easier to step aside than to go forward. It is only when you hold tight to the commitment you made to Jesus to follow Him that will get you through.

Commitment to Christ gives you many things. First, it gives you assurance of your future. It is because Christ rose from the dead that we are able to be assured of our future. You can find in any other religion in the world, dead men. And it is not just religion that people look to for hope for their future. Buddha; Mohammad; Socrates; Greek gods; all dead or fantasy. Only in Christianity do you have a man who died, rose again, and lives today. Without miracles and the resurrection of Jesus, Christianity would only be able to claim what other religions claim. But it is through the miracle of God and the resurrection of Jesus that we can have assurance today.

It isn't just in the scriptures that we find the truth of Jesus' life. History bears out the circumstances. Some want to deny God's word. It becomes much more difficult for them to deny history. Factors that only produce minimal evidence for things have a number of examples for God's word. Whether it is through archaeological or written testimony, we find a number of expressions of different evidences throughout history.

When we make a commitment, we know that Christ is right there going through the fire of life with us. Just like Peter following Christ and watching him during his trial, we too can be warmed by the fire. We, like Shadrack, Meshack and Abednego, are not alone in the fire. But when things heat up in our lives, like these three, we must remember we can burn or be saved. Either way we have committed to follow Jesus. We must remember Christ by our side no matter the outcome.

In making a commitment, I believe we often forget that we do not always win. There are only three spots on the Olympic winners stand. Many more compete but not everyone can win. Every person there has committed to their craft. The reputations of nations can lie in the hands of individuals brave enough to follow through. People throughout the world are cheering for a person because they are there to represent a nation. Although the individuals are there for themselves and to be the best they can be, they are also there as representatives.

As Christians we do the same. We commit to Christ for ourselves, but we are here so that others can cheer for Him. We must be the best representative we can be whether we win or lose. People will be disappointed. Nations may be disappointed. But, when we give all that we have and do the best we can, then the glory will be God's.

Commitment to Christ can take on many forms. They can be as varied as the individuals. Depending on what Christ calls you to do, will decide the direction of your commitment.

You may simply be called as a follower. Being a follower of Christ includes the commitment to prayer, worship and study. Without those things, you cannot grow your relationship. At the very least, your acceptance of Jesus into your heart, sets you in a relationship. Every relationship requires the commitment to communicate with one another. One of the ways in which Christ has afforded us the opportunity to communicate is through scripture. The Holy Bible is a living book. What I mean by that is that it teaches you and your understanding can change and grow. You can read the same verse that you studied years before and find new meaning. You can find refreshment and encouragement in scripture.

God's word is always uplifting, even when it brings conviction. Finding conviction in the Holy Bible will lift you from your current position to a higher position. If ever you are feeling condemned by scripture, you will need to re-evaluate your commitment. Condemnation is something that Satan brings to tear you down. Conviction is God's way of helping you make a better you. He never brings you to condemnation or to tear you down.

The commitment you make to Jesus may call you to be a Missionary. Your desire to help others to grow in Christ may be elevated. Being called as a missionary does not mean you will travel to foreign lands. It might, but it does not have to. There are many local missions. It could be your mission to council with others and help deliver them from addiction. Maybe your mission is to pray for young girls trapped in sex trafficking and help them find a way out. You could be the one that ministers to women with unplanned pregnancies. There are lots of local missions.

Being a missionary might call you away to foreign lands. It could mean living with natives to translate scriptures into their language. It could mean teaching people about Christ in very dangerous surroundings. It could be helping to build communities or homes for safer surroundings. It could be bringing healing to a body or mind. Whatever the mission God calls you to, he will equip you for, if he has not already equipped you. All the while, you are still called as a follower, to build your relationship through prayer and study.

It is important to remember too that in building a prayer life, what prayer is not. It is not begging God. It is not having God as a sugar daddy to provide your every whim. Prayer is a type of communication. It is knowing and understanding who God is and letting him know who you are. It is easy to forget that He already knows our every thought and attitude. It is sometimes allowing God to show us those things within ourselves that draws us closer to Him. Prayer is letting God know what we want and trusting that He knows what is best. Prayer is not a one-way street but is a two-way street.

God may call you to be an Evangelist. The desire for others to know God may become an overwhelming compulsion for you. Being the next Billy Graham could be your calling, but it could also be that He places everyone you meet on your heart to witness His love. Whether you are at work or traveling from church to church, you may see God's heart of love for your fellow man.

Your mission or calling could be to teach God's word to others. You might head up a Sunday School class or lead a small group at church or in a home. Maybe you will mentor people one on one. You could be called to write a devotional. Maybe God will give you a platform in the community to share His word with clubs or corporations. Maybe he will place you in a school to teach and be a Christian example to students.

Your calling could be to pastor. This might be to thousands, or it might be to a handful of believers. No matter the size, God will put you where He feels you are most useful. The hours spent studying God's word will far outweigh the time for a given presentation. You can be placed to pray for the sick and listen to your congregation gripe and complain. You could be faced with decisions that have nothing to do with promoting God's word. Every circumstance that faces a pastor includes a person that God loves and needs someone with compassion to be there for Him.

As the old saying goes, it is not the qualified that are called, but the called that God qualifies. It is important to be willing to step forward out of obedience because you see God's call on your life.

Your greatest satisfaction and joy will come in your obedience to Christ. Even if you fall on your face, or feel you have failed, it could be one step in Jesus' qualifying you for the position he has called you to. We all fail in our endeavors. Scripture guarantees us struggles not success in our own desires.

In Quiet and Solitude

In quiet and solitude, I wait for you
To hear your voice alone
While the world around me is roaring
Here I sit at the throne

Other voices daily will clamor
For my attention they seek
Desiring help through circumstance
But alas, I am too weak

At times I grow impatient
For a word just for me
Selfishly crying as the world does
When I should be on my knees

You Lord have the answers
To life and how to live
It is love and grace and forgiveness
That you have asked us to give

As I sit here humbly in your presence
Desiring to know your heart
Give me the wisdom and patience
That I may do my part

Setting aside distractions
To sit quietly in this day
To hear the voice of my Savior
As I'm bowed here to pray.

Questions to Ponder

1. How deep is your commitment?

    _____

    _____

2. Do you need to work harder in your commitment to Jesus?

    _____

    _____

3. Do you feel you are growing in prayer?

    _____

    _____

4. What other ways have you tried to communicate?

    _____

    _____

5. Do you believe you are learning more about scriptures through study?

    _____

    _____

6. Do you find it hard to be obedient to Christ?

_____

_____

7. Is there a specific call on your life that you need to fulfill?

_____

_____

8. Where have you failed in your endeavors?

_____

_____

CHAPTER TWELVE
GUIDANCE AND CONFUSING THE ENEMY

||||||||||||||||||||||||||||||||||||||||||||||||||||||||||||||||||||||||||||||||||||||||||||||||||||||||||||||||||||||||||||||||||||||||

GOD AS A CLOUD BY DAY AND FIRE BY NIGHT

". [21] And Jehovah went before them by day in a pillar of cloud, to lead them the way, and by night in a pillar of fire, to give them light; that they might go by day and by night: [22] [a] the pillar of cloud by day, and the pillar of fire by night, departed not from before the people. 14 And Jehovah spake unto Moses, saying, [2] Speak unto the children of Israel, that they turn back and encamp before Pi-hahiroth, between Migdol and the sea, before Baal-zephon: over against it shall ye encamp by the sea. [3] And Pharaoh will say of the children of Israel, They are entangled in the land, the wilderness hath shut them in. [4] And I will [b] harden Pharaoh's heart, and he shall follow after them; and I will get me honor upon Pharaoh, and upon all his host; and the Egyptians shall know that I am Jehovah. And they did so." (Exodus 13:21 - 14:4)

DIRECTION VS. CONFUSION

Obviously from the first statement in this passage, we see God's guidance for His people. He never left His position day or night. He was there to give them the necessary direction. In the same way He is always there for us. *"as I was with Moses, so I will be with thee; I will not fail thee, nor forsake thee.." (Joshua 1:5b)*

God's presence was not only a sign and guide for the people of Israel, but it was also very practical. God appeared as a cloud by day to shield His people from the harsh desert heat. His cloud shielded the people as it guided them. But the desert can become quite cold after the sun goes down. Therefore, God's pillar of fire provided the warmth and light needed during the cold, dark nights. From this we can see God's direction, protection and light for those who follow Him.

No matter where we end up, God takes our circumstances into consideration. Although we can feel uncomfortable with the surroundings we encounter, we can always know that God has already figures out what is needed to take us beyond those circumstances.

The place where God led the Jewish slaves was a place where they could be trapped. By all appearances, this was not the wisest of places to camp. It was a place of vulnerability. Scripture shows us how God uses the foolish things of the world to confound the wise. Remember it is important to see how God does not allow circumstances to dictate an outcome. Here is a perfect example. God led the people in what **appeared** to be confusion and certain destruction. Not only did he lead them there, He made their enemy aware of their vulnerability. The Egyptians must have thought inexperience was normal for such an enemy. Such ignorance would be an easy target to overcome. To the outside, the Jews appeared to be foolish, not knowing where they were going.

Many times, we feel like we are in a state of confusion, wandering around unsure where we need to be. But the cloud of the Lord and the fire of His Spirit are still with us. We must still follow Him.

Just as the Lord used the circumstances of the Jewish people to confuse the enemy and allow him to feel confident of victory, so it is true for us. I am sure many of those being delivered from Egypt were confused as to God's direction. They knew Pharaoh's army was pursuing them and that they were camped at a dead end. They grumbled at Moses. They lay blame for their imminent destruction at his feet. I fear today that many Godly pastors receive great blame for God taking His people to their place of deliverance.

I am sure Pharaoh, after experiencing such a great defeat, was ready for revenge. I know many people have asked why God would harden Pharaoh's heart. However, I believe that simply giving him knowledge of the circumstances was enough. Those who reject God are easily and quickly subject to their own desires. For someone angry and bent on revenge, hardness is only a heartbeat away.

Complete deliverance of God's people was dependent on Pharaoh's cooperation, either through his resignation to and acknowledgement of God's position and power or through his own destruction. He chose destruction when he decided to stand against God.

Pharaoh was a man of power, and even in the face of God, he was not willing to let go of that power. A pharaoh was considered by many to be a god. This man obviously bought into that image. Experiencing a devastating defeat must have been humiliating for him. But he did not want to acknowledge or turn to the one true God. He was not willing to change. He only wanted the discomfort of the circumstances to change.

He may have been facing a nation on the verge of rebellion because God had brought plague after plague upon them. Also, now the land had been stripped of its slaves and many of its resources. Did Pharaoh feel he was about to lose his power? Could rebellion destroy him? To secure his own position, he had to salvage as much power, prestige and pride as possible. So, when he was handed what appeared to be a certain victory, he could not resist.

If God had left this unrestrained man to his own devices, Pharaoh could have possibly convinced the Egyptian people that he alone had rid the country of the Israelites – that it was not God's doing. But by allowing Pharaoh to pursue them, God was able to demonstrate that no <u>man</u> can thwart God's plans. And God received all the glory for the salvation of His people.

This is a great example of the importance of following God and trusting Him, even when it causes confusion or unpleasant circumstances. I know I am not alone in that there have been many times in my life – sometimes for years – where I have felt alone and lost in the desert, not knowing where God was taking me. When we are in those circumstances, it is important to press into God in prayer and seek His direction and to trust Him with our uncertainty. His deliverance will come, though most likely, not as we expect.

I must admit that my perception comes more from hindsight than from foresight. Even though as in this passage of Scripture, God tells us what is going to happen, our perception is skewed because God's thoughts are higher than our thoughts and His ways higher than our ways.

GUIDANCE

Another thing the cloud and pillar in this Scripture shows us is that it confused the enemy. We all have enemies, even the best-loved people. Even Jesus had enemies.

Enemies come in all shapes and sizes. Let's look at Moses. His enemy was Pharaoh, whose heart was against him. Pharaoh was from the same household where Moses was raised! These were not strangers who disliked one another. The former Pharaoh's daughter raised Moses. So, this man that was now ruler of Egypt and from whom Moses sought to release his people, was like a brother.

Jealousy and rivalry among siblings have long been a problem. When we add the number of blended families we see in our society today, and the conflicts created by them, we can clearly understand how Moses and Pharaoh clashed. After letting Moses and the Israelites leave, do you not think Pharaoh was upset because he felt manipulated and embarrassed? How often do we turn our anger for our own decisions against those we gave our word?

But God will not be steered away from the course He has set. He will confuse the enemy in such a way that in the end, God gets the glory. When all is said and done, others will know He is Lord. So, knowing that, we can put our trust and confidence in God, we can keep our eyes on following Him because we remember what He has told us.

Personal Experience

Only after I began to learn more about Jesus could I look back on my life and see how God's presence had always been with me. When I look back now, I see the directions God has taken me in my life without my conscious awareness. My experience has given me a much greater under-standing than I ever could have had earlier.

I am reminded of how God began to teach me his word. Although I had been saved, I was ignorant of His word. There were two of us that started a new job on the same day. We were the only two in this one room all day doing calculations for quarterly reports. We spent a lot of time talking and she and I did not have the same spiritual inter-pretations. She knew far more about God's word than I did. She would make these statements that I just felt were outrageous. Since I am a bit stubborn and wanting to prove that I was right, I would go home and dig through my Bible and find the verse she was talking about. I admit that she, more often than not, had a very valid point. Although I did not always agree with her interpretation of a scripture, God used her to teach me about His word and how to trust Him more. This was steel sharpening steel.

When I stand in a cloudy place, unsure of the future, I now know it is in following God that I will reach my destination. It is important to remember that God has taken people both young and old and used them for His purposes. Our job is to follow, trusting that God will provide and receive all the glory.

Just as the Israelites immediately saw how God rescued them and destroyed their enemy, it also took many years before they saw the Promised Land. At times, we can immediately see God's hand in our lives. Other times, even though time may seem to interfere, it is import-ant for us to remember that God's timing is perfect. Our impatience will not make things move faster or better. It is through our faith and patience that we will see the promises of God. And yes, sometimes that means years of waiting.

Remain faithful and hopeful. That faith and hope can be seen by others. It could be one of them that God needs to reach before fulfilling

His promise to you. I am always amazed when someone tells me they see faith or strength in me, especially during those times where I feel lost. But that intangible insight comes from God and is a glimpse of His glory that others see through you.

When Jesus ask the disciples who they thought He was, the response from Peter was that Jesus was the Messiah. *"Jesus replied, "Blessed are you, Simon son of Jonah, for this was not revealed to you by flesh and blood, but by my Father in heaven."* (Matthew 16:17) God is the one that gives us glimpses of truth.

It is important to keep in mind that as Christians, we listen to what God is saying, through His word, circumstances and that still, small voice we hear within our heart. He will make clear to us His plans. Even when, like the Jewish people, we do not understand how, when or why something is going to work, we can trust in His promises to us. Hebrews 11:1 tells us, "Now faith is [a]assurance of *things* hoped for, a [b]conviction of things not seen.." I believe the most important word here is "**Now**"! Keeping faithful to what God has said will always bring you through the circumstances that appear to be contrary. Keeping faith **now** will help you continue in the hope you need to sustain you. And when you think all your faith is fading, stir up hope, for that is the evidence you need.

The Spirit of God

I'm glad your Spirit is with me.
I can feel it all around
And in this quiet and peaceful time
It is a beautiful sound.

I hear your voice
And feel you near
I can see your face
Though you be not here.

Only a friend who is
As close as you
Could be so near
When I need you.

QUESTIONS TO PONDER

1. Are you ever confused by God's word?

   _____

   _____

2. Do you have promises from God that you believe are unfulfilled?

   _____

   _____

3. How does God guide you?

   _____

   _____

4. Have you been confused by God's guidance?

   _____

   _____

5. Have you argued with God from the worlds view point that something is foolish?

   _____

   _____

6. When do you know of a time when others were able to see God working in or through you?

_____

_____

7. Can you see yourself the same way God sees you?

_____

_____

8. Has waiting on God's promise been difficult?

_____

_____

CHAPTER THIRTEEN
WAITING

||||||||||||||||||||||||||||||||||||||||||||||||||||||||||||||||||||||||||||||||||||||||||||||||||||||||||||||||||||

*"And when forty years were fulfilled, an angel ap-
peared to him in the wilderness of mount Sinai, in a
flame of fire in a bush."* Acts 7:30

Waiting is hard. We naturally want things when we want them. We
are not usually prepared to wait. There was a time when waiting was a
more expected response to things. Credit was not so readily available,
and people waited to purchase something until they had saved the
money to make the purchase. Sometimes this meant years. Luxuries were
items that might take decades to save for their purchase. Things were
not produced "on demand". Waiting for something was a more natural
response. Immediate gratification was not a concept that everyone held
as the standard operating procedure in all matters.

The following dialogue was in the movie "God's Not Dead, Light in
the Darkness." I watched this movie and thought this particular passage
profound.

"John (the Baptist) needed to doubt."
"Why?"
"Because uncertainty leads to the pursuit of truth. I
know it hurts to be in the fire, and as painful and con-
fusing as all of this is, it just might be exactly where God
wants you right now."

The pursuit of truth can be difficult. We can struggle with our own
responses and question our motives, especially if we are struggling or are
questioning God. We somehow feel that by wondering or questioning
God we have somehow committed a great sin. Instead of seeking God's
direction we think of Him differently, depending upon what we are

feeling at the moment. If we feel loved and appreciated by God, we treat Him like a friend or our sugar daddy in the sky. If we are feeling used or abandoned, we tend to think of Him as a big ogre. Both ideas are wrong.

We forget that Jacob struggled. Because of his circumstances, Jacob spent a whole night struggling with God. He would not let go because he wanted to know that he had God's blessing. We tend to struggle but forget to ask God for His blessing and hold on until we know we have it. Being told and thinking that something is true does not get it into our heart and beliefs. Like Jacob, we need to have a response, that will not let go. We need to allow ourselves, even through desperate circumstances, to spend time in prayer and wrestling with our misgivings.

I wish I could remember the name of the movie I recently watched, but I do remember the lesson it taught me. The movie talked about how things are done FOR us and not TO us. I thought, "Wow". What a concept that was. I have read and quote the scripture telling us that God does all things for the good of those called according to His riches in glory, but the day I watched that movie, it began to make more sense to me. It thought of Joseph. I am sure he did not think God was doing anything **for** him as he sat in prison after being falsely accused. This was not an overnight struggle for him. He sat in jail for a long time, but he rose and was placed in a position of authority. He was second only to the Pharoah in Egypt.

It is hard for us to believe that we can be angry with God or question him. Somehow, that feels like we have a lack of faith. Instead of seeking to know God's thoughts, we assume that not knowing is a lack of faith. I had someone tell me once, when I was upset with God to yell at Him. He already knew how I felt, and He was big enough to take it. It changed my perspective. I am now reminded of just how big a God we serve. Now and again, I have to be reminded but I do remember.

We live in a society that wants immediate answers. Society tells us we do not have to wait. We do not always understand God's motives or what He is doing. But it is not our goal to know what God is doing. It is our goal to fulfill our purpose. Not knowing what that purpose is, we must wait on God to learn. That means we must listen to what He has to say. We must trust that His choosing is not a mistake. We must be willing to obey what we know He is saying to us.

Once we understand that God has given us a promise, then it is important that we rest and wait on that promise. The answer might not come today or tomorrow. It could be years or decades before we see God's word fulfilled in our life. That does not mean He will not be faithful in what he has said to us. It is important that we remember that God is not bound by time as we are. We see things on a linear plain. God does not. He sees the whole page. We, like ants wander across the black and white spaces of the words on that page and can only see lines and spaces.

It is also important to remember we do not confuse what God tells us with lies that the enemy wants us to believe and follow. It is a lie that you can have it all now. For many people, having it now could be quite destructive to them. I read a statistic that when people win the lottery, they are often quickly broke, because they did not know how to handle money. The amount they win only gives them a temporary fix. They quickly return to their previous circumstances or end up deeper in debt. God understands who we are and what can be helpful or harmful to us. He is not our sugar daddy to give us a temporary fix. He gently persuades us in the direction we need to go. For some, that is done quickly. For those of us that have a more "willful" attitude, it could take much longer. When others are involved, it means we must also wait on God to deal with them properly.

God promised Abraham to be a blessing to all nations. He did not live to see that fulfilled. However, today we can see the blessings throughout the world that have been given because of Abraham's faithfulness. He believed God although he did not see the promise fulfilled during his life. His descendants are worldwide and too numerous to count.

Moses stood before a burning bush. He was exiled because of prior actions but he trusted God in His promise to deliver God's people. It is not always what we think is best. Moses did not want the call on his life. He pleaded with God to get someone else. However, God knew who the best man for the job was. He had known from the time of Moses birth. He placed Moses in a position not of slavery, but to have access to the Pharaoh. This access is what gave him the ability to fulfill God's promise.

The wait was not only the decades that Moses wondered in the desert with the Israeli people, it was also the decades before. The people who cried out in prayer for deliverance waited decades for the answer of a deliverer. It was the wait from Moses' time of position in the house of Pharaoh to his time exiled and standing before God on Holy ground to receive his purpose.

We often forget about our time of preparation. The time God takes to put all the pieces of our lives and the lives of others into a position perfect to fulfill His purposes. We are so anxious to have what we believe is best for us, we are not willing to face the seemingly impossible. We cannot believe our eyes when we stand before a burning bush on Holy ground and receive marching orders. Like Moses, we can be found arguing with God about what needs to be done. Waiting and obedience to God's way is not always how we see things as being best.

We certainly do not believe that struggling or hardships should be part of the process. But one thing we can count on is that whatever promise God gives will be aligned with the word of God which we already have. The devil will do his best to pervert whatever promise God gives us. His goal is to steal any hope we have for our future or the future of those around us. The devil wants us to mistrust God and will use current circumstances to convince us that waiting is a mistake. He will lie to us that we misheard God or that our wait has been too long. Anything the devil can do to distract us from the truth, he will use.

So, whether you feel you are standing in the midst of the fire like Shadrack, Meshach and Abednego, or are looking at a burning bush wondering how this could be, remember that God's word for you is faithful. He can be trusted whether it takes you forty seconds to see results, forty years, or those results come after your life. God's plan and purpose for your life is well worth waiting on, even through fiery circumstances.

Waiting for the Moment

Waiting for the moment
It finally is here
Waiting for the moment
Things are finally clear

Waiting for the moment
When hearts become alive
Waiting for the moment
Such pleasure is now mine

Waiting for the moment
No sweeter love I've known
Waiting for the moment
Your heart is now my home

Waiting for the moment
Now seems no time has passed
Waiting for the moment
My anticipations all surpassed

QUESTIONS TO PONDER

1. Are you anxious to see God's promises to you fulfilled?

   _____

   _____

2. Do you need more patience?

   _____

   _____

3. Do you know something specific that God has promised you?

   _____

   _____

4. Does your faith waiver when you wait on God?

   _____

   _____

5. How long have you waited for your promise?

   _____

   _____

6. Are you disappointed in God because you have not seen a promise fulfilled?

_____

_____

7. What do you do with your disappointment?

_____

_____

8. Does waiting make more sense to you now?

_____

_____

CHAPTER FOURTEEN
MESSENGERS

|||||||||||||||||||||||||||||||||||||||||||||||||||||||||||||||||||||||||||||||||||||||||||||||||||||||||||||||||||||||||||||||

"And of the angels he saith, Who maketh his angels winds, And his ministers a flame of fire:" Hebrews 1:7

Often, we will hear people say "Don't shoot the messenger" before they begin telling us something or just after they finish with a message. This is a sure sign that they are delivering information they believe you do not want to hear. It is something being delivered to us as a third party. There can be many reasons why the original messenger does not deliver the message himself. The statement to "not shoot the messenger" usually implies a negative impact on the one hearing it. Maybe it's the death of someone which brings great sorrow. It could be the demise of something precious or valuable to us. Whatever the reason, the results can appear to the third party as negative.

However, this is not always the case. Even in the event of a death of a loved one, we might be relieved in our grief to know that they are no longer in a condition of suffering. But the messages we want to discuss here are on a more positive note. Well, at least the final outcome will be positive.

As God gives His ministers a word for His people, He can do it with passion, placing a flame so hot within them that delivering His word will produce a fire not only within the person but also within those hearing it. As we have discussed earlier in the book, a fire can be both destructive and constructive. When hearing the truth, we are not always prepared to accept or believe what the messenger has to say. Many people reject Jesus as their Savior. That does not change the fact that He hung on a cross and died. Nor does it negate the fact that three days later he arose from the dead and lives still today? All of this was done so that we could be forgiven for our sins and live. The people who hear Gods word, who hear the truth, who listen to the history and the hope that we have in

Jesus, are not always excited to hear it. To some, it is a burning passion that begins a whole new life. To others, they only see the destruction of a life they love, and they reject it. The interesting thing about this is that whether they accept the truth or reject God's gift, there is a fiery response.

This is true for all phases of our life. When faced with truth, we either accept or reject it. I remember a time when I was counseling with my pastor that he pointed out a truth to me that I did not accept at first. I was angry. I was angry at him. It took me days to begin to understand that the truth he was pointing out in my life meant that I had to make some changes. I had to decide if I was going to continue in accepting what was detrimental to me or accept the truth and move forward in a new direction. Since we do not like change, accepting it can be difficult. I did finally decide to embrace the truth. Now that does not mean that from that point on everything went smoothly. Actually, my decision, and the changes I made affected other people. Remember how I said we do not like change? Well, no one does and my decision that affected others caused them to be angry. At that point, it was not my responsibility to make them happy. At that point, the responsibility was taken from me and placed in their hands.

Although our decisions can have an effect on others, we must accept our own responsibilities. We must allow others to accept their responsibilities. This is not always easy. In the case of someone accepting Jesus Christ as their Savior, you may find that many around them are not happy with the decision. Rejection can be an expected response by others, especially those who are close. The truth does not change. People's reactions change.

The fiery passion can be the response of both the messenger and the one receiving the message. The reason for this is because many people live in a grey zone. We do not want to see truth as black or white. We want to believe that there are areas of exception to every rule. Truth that challenges our exceptions and expectations can be difficult. Accepting a black or white truth and eliminating the varying degrees of exceptions from our thinking forces us to challenge ourselves.

One of the biggest controversies facing our society today is that of pro-life versus pro-abortion. Because we want to feel better about being on the fence with this issue, many people accept the pro-choice stance. Being pro-abortion says that you believe it is fine to kill a child at any point in a woman's pregnancy. Being pro-life means that you value life under all circumstances. Pro-choice seems to allow grey areas where you can adjust your belief and feel better about yourself. However, by accepting the grey areas and allowing room to adjust your beliefs, most people feel they are allowing others more freedom. Pro-choice does not say that "I have permission to choose life and death." Pro-choice says "A woman has the right to choose for herself." The option becomes impersonal. It avoids committing to believing you value life or you accept killing a child. The truth is the choice is personal.

On this one issue, being pro-choice does not actually mean you are removing a personal decision. It means that you leave your options open in case you have to make a personal decision. If you are pro-choice, it comes down to actually accepting the killing of a child. It means if you accept that it is okay for others to kill a baby in the mother's womb, then they must accept it if you have to make that same decision. It means that you can allow circumstances to dictate your decision and not the black and while truth you are faced with.

Accepting the truth challenges your personal opinion. Fence sitting is extremely uncomfortable when it comes to facing reality. In the case of a pro-life or pro-abortion position, facing your own beliefs hits home when you are faced with a decision in your own life. If this were not the case, there would not be Pregnancy Resource Centers and abortion clinics throughout our nation. When faced with an unexpected or unwanted pregnancy, it takes courage for a girl to walk into one of these places and face herself. Abortion clinics are there to make money and they may not give you the whole truth. Pregnancy Resource Centers are there to help and you are more likely to get the whole truth. Either way, you must make a personal choice.

It is important for volunteers at the Pregnancy Resource Center's to remember that the decision still remains with the woman who is pregnant. Some pro-life people have an agenda to simply save lives. They can induce as much pressure on a woman as someone wanting her to abort her child. If both sides would remember it is the decision of that girl and she must live with her decision. Their responsibility is simply to love the person through their decision and allow her to live with that decision. This takes a great deal of compassion.

It is true for both parents of the child. Men wanting to avoid their own responsibility can cause a great deal of pressure on the mother. Mothers wanting fathers to accept their decisions can come at odds with them. Anger can be the result on both parents' side. Compassion and love are what will get both through the process. Respecting the opinion of the other partner and realizing they too must face consequences for their decision goes a long way.

Compassion and love need to be the driving factors in any message. The passionate fire God can place within someone for delivering a message must not overstep the bounds of personal responsibility. I'm reminded of Jonah. He did everything he knew how to avoid God's call on his life. He actually headed in the other direction from a people that he did not like. His argument with God was that if he went, the people of Neveah would repent. That was God's purpose in sending him there. But his own prejudice and negative passion for the people drove him in the opposite direction. It was God's loving compassion that brought Jonah to speak to the people of Neveah. Jonah was angry about what God wanted him to do. But, when faced with the truth of his own prejudices, his choice was for the salvation of a nation.

We tend to forget about the responsibility of allowing others to live with their decision. We want to "fix" things. I'm afraid that control is a better description of what we want. We want people to think and react as we would. I am grateful that the founding fathers of the United States were not so short sighted. They embraced the responsibility of others in our Constitution. They allowed for disagreements by giving us freedom of speech, freedom of the press and freedom of religion. Although it might appear easier to demand that an atheist accept Christ, it would have been a sham. Many might profess to have accepted Jesus but still hold contempt in their hearts. Without two or more sides, we would not have more than one political party. If the media were required to only report what they were told, we would not be allowed to hear the truth or to decide for ourselves what we want to believe.

Today we see this split in our information and society. We see people divided in ideas and information. Instead of being God's messenger and spreading His word, we take our own side. We believe whichever side we stand on and expect everyone else to fall in line with our thinking. The media works to manipulate others to think their way. We sometimes forget that we live in a free society and allow the messengers to manipulate us instead of informing us.

Our actions are a result of our thinking and beliefs. What is called "peer pressure" when we are young and in school, never goes away. It changes. How those around us look at things allows for pressure to be placed on our own lives. Instead of trusting God and obeying His laws, we tend to pick a side. How we think and believe brings the consequences we face in our lives. Facing those consequences is the responsibility we accept. Some may want to avoid responsibility by playing the "ignore it and it will go away" game. That, in itself, is a decision. Every decision brings with it, consequences and responsibility. We may delay action, but we will never avoid it entirely.

Ministers have a different type of pressure and responsibility. Although the desire to please others is always present for everyone, it is heightened for ministers. They stand before a diverse group of people, all with different beliefs and understanding. They receive pressure from each one to "perform" to the expectations each holds. With every sermon or private conversation, they risk making someone angry. This is not a good recipe for pleasing people. The real truth is that these ministers only have one that they must please. That is God the Father who has called them to their position. The more they seek His will and purpose, the more confidence they will have when presenting His message. The more they study God's word and pray over the meaning and the message, the more pleasing they will be to the Father.

Again, we are faced with the responsibility of what to do with a message. If a minister allows those receiving God's message to taint his words, the message can be destructive. It can be hurtful for him and even for the person receiving the message. If he allows God's message to speak for him, the responsibility is shifted back to the listener. We do not want to shoot the messenger. We want God's word, spoken, or written to be received in prayer to touch our lives.

Not all messages come through pastors. That is our first thought. Messages can also come through prayer or a lay person. It is not actually the pastor's job to only give messages and help people. It is his job to train others to be God's disciples. Again, and again we hear stories about how people who have listened to God have delivered encouragement or given material needs to strangers. I can testify that on more than one occasion, I have been doing one thing when God popped into my head and gave me a message. However unexpected, it has always been relevant. At this point, obedience is paramount. I must confess that I have not always been obedient. Each of those time of rebellion, I have regretted.

Some messages come through angels. Scriptures tell us we can be unaware of the presence of an angel. Angels are God's messengers. We might think of them as babies with wings sitting on clouds. We might picture them as a guardian on our behalf. We might believe that they are loved ones who receive wings after they die. Whatever our perception or what others have caused us to believe, they can be powerful messengers for God. I cannot begin to explain how or why God uses angels to give us messages. I simply take it on faith because it is written in the Bible.

Without listening to the messengers around us, our responsibility can lead us to isolation and destruction. Never condemning, God encourages us to examine our lives and to choose what He has for us. Accepting responsibility for ourselves is a decision we must each make at some point in our life. If we do not listen and make our own decisions, we are controlled. That control can be from God, individuals around us, from society or from the devil. We want that control to be in the hands of God. He is the one that we must ultimately answer to. Anyone else, holds a false place of authority over us.

We are bombarded with messages from all types of sources. It is how we accept those messages, and which voices we follow that will decide who we follow. Will we see the black and white of truth or will we embrace the shades of gray that dull our world?

It is important that angels and pastors are not the only messengers God has appointed. We each have a responsibility to others. Whether it is through encouragement or truth. We have a responsibility to spread God's truth. From that point when we except Jesus as our savior, it is our responsibility to learn and to teach. Just as a child learns to walk, we much learn to step out in God's word. It is not the responsibility of the pastor to go into all the world. It is his responsibility to train and teach each of us to go. It is our responsibility to step forward and go into all the world.

Hazy Days

How can my heart lie to me?
These feeling seem so true
But what's aroused inside of me
Has come from out of the blue

My mind is trying to wrap around
The confusion that is there
The Want within the emotion
To the truth I seem to fear

What's right or wrong; true or false
Alludes my common sense
Only the nagging of my own will
Seems to call and to persist

Lord, I need you to surround me
To set my mind at ease
Come and settle my emotions
Please come and bring your peace

Keep my mind stayed on you.
My heart filled with praise.
May I continue in your graces
Let your Spirit clear the haze.

QUESTIONS TO PONDER

1. Who do you allow to speak into your life?

_____

_____

2. Where do you need to make a decision to take responsibility?

_____

_____

3. How can you let go and allow someone else their own responsibility?

_____

_____

4. What areas can you pinpoint that have too many shades of grey?

_____

_____

5. Do you ever argue with God?

_____

_____

6. Have you ever won an argument with God?

_____

_____

7. How have you changed after being angry about something?

_____

_____

8. Are you equipped to go into the world?

_____

_____

9. Are you equipped to teach others?

_____

_____

10. What do you need to faithfully present the message you have?

_____

_____

CHAPTER FIFTEEN
JUDGEMENT AND REVENGE

||||||||||||||||||||||||||||||||||||||||||||||||||||||||||||||||||||||||||||||||||||||||||||||||||||||||||||||||||||||||||||||||||

> *⁵ All this is evidence that God's judgment is right, and as a result you will be counted worthy of the kingdom of God, for which you are suffering. ⁶ God is just: He will pay back trouble to those who trouble you ⁷ and give relief to you who are troubled, and to us as well. This will happen when the Lord Jesus is revealed from heaven in blazing fire with his powerful angels. ⁸ He will punish those who do not know God and do not obey the gospel of our Lord Jesus. ⁹ They will be punished with everlasting destruction and shut out from the presence of the Lord and from the glory of his might ¹⁰ on the day he comes to be glorified in his holy people and to be marveled at among all those who have believed. This includes you, because you believed our testimony to you.* 2 Thessalonians 1:5-10

JUDGEMENT:

We learn from this passage of scripture that judgment is something that God does. He has the exclusive right and ability to see both our actions and our intensions in any situation. He judges us rightly. God's ability to see our hearts and to reveal them to us is amazing.

God looks at those intentions and filters them not through feelings but through the blood of Jesus. If we are found as someone who has accepted Jesus Christ as our savior, our sin is filtered out and we are found to be worthy. Although our actions may be something that we take to Jesus and place at His feet at the cross, we can be found worthy by God. It is not our actions, but the action Jesus took to absolve us of our sins.

There is a worship song that says it is not our actions but those of Jesus that count. God counts our sins as those covered by the death and blood shed of His son. That is why it is important that we always take our circumstances, emotions, and actions to Jesus to determine our actions.

Christ has a purpose for each of us. He has also given each of us a unique personality to fulfill that purpose. Personally, I am a shy introvert. For some strange reason, I can stand before a crowd and have no problem with it. However, if you ask me to enter a room and mingle, I will have a hard time with that. Give me a corner and let someone come over to talk and I am good. That is my unique personality. You may have a hard time speaking in front of people, but networking could be a breeze for you. That is your unique personality.

Many try to explain our different personalities from a cookie cutter. The truth is that those cookie cutter explanations cannot account for the subtle differences we each have. Maybe you are right brain or left brain; you could be an A personality or an extrovert, or maybe you are just weird. Those very labels can account for the big differences we each have. However, as we each have unique fingerprints, we each have unique personalities.

Dealing with and knowing your unique personality and purpose in life is important, because change is the one thing we can always count on. There will always be a change in our personality as we grow and mature. God is not surprised by the changes we make or the speed at which we mature. His purpose in our life will adjust as we change. He will always use us right where we are.

As a woman living in the age of feminist upheaval, I have often wrestled with my place. I have learned some things as I have studied God's word. First thing I have learned is that as a woman, we are important to God. We are no more important than men, nor are we less important. We simply have different roles. God has placed a hierarchy in place. Since Adam and Eve, God has been the head and a covering. Men are the next covering but for those of us that do not have a male covering in our lives, God is still our covering.

Another lesson I have learned is that God is no respecter of persons. I recently was studying four women in the lineage of Christ. Each has a place in scripture that we see and study today. Although the lineage of Christ traces through men, we can find each of these women in the lives of those men. Tamar, Rehab, Ruth and Bathsheba can all be found having an impact. Prostitutes, widows, and shamed women have a major role in the life of Christ. These are the people Christ came to save. These are the people we read in scripture that he associated with and talked directly to.

We are no different. Our sins are His to judge. Whether we consider ourselves as being righteous or sinful, there are sins in our lives that can only be judged justly by God. We do not want to be found like the Pharisees, judging others with our own expectations and interpretations of scripture. We must not think too highly of ourselves, lest we find ourselves ignoring what God is trying to show us in our own hearts.

Trying to judge another with our own filters of experience can only bring a different result from each person in our life. Someone who knows my secrets and feelings can judge me quite differently from someone who knows very little about me. They are just as bad as the one who tries to judge without knowing. We are not able to see the hearts of others. Only God has that unique ability. He alone can judge and be just.

REVENGE

So often we feel that we have been wronged or unjustly judged for something. We want to place our feelings of hurt or sadness or anger on someone other than ourselves. We do not like the feeling and want to rid ourselves of it. The circumstances do not matter much. We feel offended. We always feel that offenses are due to the actions or words of someone else. Rarely are we willing to "take the blame" or accept "responsibility" for what has been done.

However, many times it is our own doing. We are at fault for circumstances that have brought us harm. Maybe we previously offended someone, and they are retaliating. Maybe we have had expectations that were unrealistic for ourselves or someone else, and reality is too difficult to face. We do not wish to be at fault but to fault others. There are times that the offense is not our doing. It is fully on the shoulders of someone else. Our offense is justified and reasonable. We know we have every right to seek revenge for being treated so horribly.

At these times, the circumstances that stand in our face are of no consequence. It is the desire of our heart to make the offending party as miserable as we are feeling. Whether we are to blame or someone else, we want revenge. However, the reality is that God has called us to a higher standard. We are to turn the other cheek, not seek revenge. Since we are made in God's image, he expects us to rise above our humanity, trust in Him and react in a Holy manner.

This of course is not our first reaction. Anger can rise us within us for being offended. We can strike out at someone because we are angry. The offender may be our target of anger. The fiery darts we spew may be directed at the offending party. However, they may also be spewed at an innocent by-stander. Although it is not our intention to be angry with anyone else, we too can be the offender to someone else because of our reactions. This can cause a chain reaction of injury all because we were unwilling to take our anger to the Lord instead of first reacting from our emotions.

Anger in and of itself is not wrong. Jesus was angry when he turned over the tables of the merchants and moneychangers in the temple. The word of God tells us to be angry and sin not. It is actually what we do with our anger that matters. It is not our job to spew it at others, but to first take it to the Lord. That reaction time may take a while, or it may take seconds. Knowing our emotions and the reasons behind them can be different for different people. But it is important to remember that we do not live by emotions. They can, and often do, lie to us about circumstances.

People who have over-reacted with their emotions, ignored or stuffed them for an extended period will have a harder time of processing. It is not always an easy process to know why you are having a particular emotion arise.

If hurt wells up within you and tears flow down your face, it could be because of misplaced or misdirected expectations. It could be because you were genuinely hurt. It could also be because you are angry but have stuffed that feeling so long you can no longer feel it as anger. The truth can be true in reverse. We may spew anger when the truth is that we are feeling very hurt and have stuffed that feeling away.

We can do the same thing with many emotions. People will laugh when hurting because they are used to putting on that mask to hide their feelings from others. Joy can produce tears instead of a smile. Fear can hide behind a smile. As wide as the range of emotions spans, so do the ways in which we put up masks to hide those feelings. The problem in doing that is that it is not always others that we hide those feelings from. We hide them from ourselves so long that we can no longer identify them.

The best defense is of course to always know what you are feeling and how to respond in an appropriate manner. Knowing our emotions is important if we are to learn to take them to the Lord. Knowing that sounds quite simple. But, knowing and doing are very different and it is rare that we do both.

We are not alone in our desire to justify things. Even the disciples, those who were next to the Lord and learned daily from him for years had questions. When they were headed to Jerusalem where Christ would be crucified, they were opposed by the Samaritans. James and John wanted a quick solution.

> *"And when his disciples James and John saw this, they said, Lord, wilt thou that we bid fire to come down from heaven, and consume them?" (Luke 9:54)*

Christ was the one who sought a different route and went to another city. This just shows us that it is important that we always take our feelings, our trials and questions to the Lord. Our own thinking is not always what is right. God has another way. That way is one of love and compassion.

We find in the book of Romans that love and compassion can often be a much more difficult experience for our enemies than anything we can contrive. It says:

> *"But if thine enemy hunger, feed him; if he thirst, give him to drink: for in so doing thou shalt heap coals of fire upon his head."* (Romans 12:20)

Besides being God's remedy to a solution, it can be an example to others. The coals that are often heaped upon another can be the pangs of guilt they see in themselves. Although we can often want to heap coals for our own revenge, it is not our place to show them their errors. It is God's alone. He is the only one that can justly access a situation and see the hearts of all involved.

That means it is important that we not seek revenge but know our own heart and feelings. We must seek God in order to know our emotions and to act in accordance with His will and purpose. When we step outside those parameters, what is our solution to seeking judgment or revenge for those that we feel have wronged us? There is only one solution, and it is the one that Jesus Christ demonstrated on the cross. It is forgiveness.

A Man After God's Own Heart

There aren't many like him today
Men who love
Men of peace
He is a man after God's Own Heart

He is a man of compassion
A man who is gentle
A man who listens
He is a man after God's Own Heart

Not a great man of power
But feared by those who are
His power is in forgiveness
He's a man after God's Own Heart

Talented and creative he builds with his hands
He shares football with his wife
And serves her the best he can
He's a man after God's Own Heart

The head of his family and head of his home
Watches over the widows and orphans
Mother, Sister and more
He's a man after God's Own Heart

Life has thrown him many a curve
He rolls with the punches
Let's the Lord lead his way
He's a man after God's Own Heart

Forgetting what's past
He presses on toward the mark
Always holding high the standard
He's a man after God's Own Heart

QUESTIONS TO PONDER

1. What situations have you found yourself in where you have put on a mask?

   _____

   _____

2. What unique traits do you believe God has given you to fulfill His purpose?

   _____

   _____

3. Is there someone you would like to repay with revenge?

   _____

   _____

4. Are you able to easily identify your feelings or does it take you time to figure out what you feel?

   _____

   _____

5. How have your feeling lied to you?

_____

_____

6. Is there someone you need to forgive for an offense?

_____

_____

7. Is there something you need to forgive yourself for?

_____

_____

8. Is there someone you see differently from the way God sees them?

_____

_____

CHAPTER SIXTEEN
POWER IN GOD'S PRESENCE

||||||||||||||||||||||||||||||||||||||||||||||||||||||||||||||||||||||||||||||||||||||||||||||||||||||||||||||||||||||||||||||

There is a great deal of satisfaction in knowing that God is an all-powerful God. Understanding it is not our own power that accomplishes things, but it is through God. The scriptures tell us that when we are weak, he is strong. It is that understanding that helps us through all that we must accomplish.

> *"And there appeared unto them tongues parting asunder, like as of fire; and it sat upon each one of them."* Acts 2:3

Accepting and believing God's power is a big step in our faith. As the early church gathered together, it was evident to all those around them that the Holy Spirit had fallen upon them. That is not something that cannot happen today. We need to be beacons in the darkness for others to see Christ. Once the Holy Spirit has fallen upon you, you must be a beacon of hope for others to see.

I heard a story several years ago about a church that was meeting and worshiping God. They were so focused on God that the corporate manifestation was enormous. The power of God manifested in such fire that someone outside thought the building was burning and called the fire department. They showed up looking for the fire and wondering why someone had reported the building burning.

We depend upon God to show up. The intensity of His power and the fire in our lives is something that can be seen by others even when they do not understand it. When the church was seen in the Book of Acts, the people did not have literal flames coming from their heads. However, those that saw them recognized the burning heart of Jesus through them. It was apparent that Christ was present with them.

Even today, we hear stories about how criminals are turned away from people because of someone speaking out in Jesus' name. The power of God on them cannot be resisted. What can cause such faithfulness and power? It is the power God manifests when we keep our focus on Him. It is the fire of the Holy Spirit dominating our lives.

Far too often, we try to accomplish things under our own power. We will work very hard to make things happen. We do this because we believe it is the best thing at the time. We do it because someone told us that was the direction we needed to go. We do it because we research books and the internet and magazines and anything else so we can be knowledgeable about a subject. We can work ourselves into a frenzy trying to make something happen or to do something just the right way.

Our intensions can be honorable and acceptable. However, our focus can be way off. Although we never want to neglect learning, we also do not want to neglect focusing on God. We do many things out of knowledge and there are many things we cannot do without it. However, if that knowledge leads us into an area where God has not meant for us to go, we are not going to accomplish the purpose He has for us in our life. We are out to accomplish our own purpose.

The saying "You can do anything you put your mind to." is both correct and incorrect. It is incorrect because it leaves God out of the equation. We are not created to do anything we think about. The reason it is correct is because God has given each of us a personality that is bent toward accomplishing the purpose in life He has set out for us. He has given us the desire and drive to do things within His plan. We still need to study and show ourselves approved for the task. We still need to work toward the goals. We still need to seek God's will in the circumstances. But it is only through the power of God anything is accomplished.

Moses was a man slow of speech. He did not feel adequate to the task God had before him. However, God had long before placed him in the house of Pharaoh. He had grown up learning the ways of the elite in Egypt and not how a slave lived. He knew these people. Where a slave could never have had the access he had, it was still not under his own power that Moses was able to lead the Jewish people out of slavery.

Moses did not turn the Nile to blood nor initiate any of the other plagues that fell upon Egypt. That was all done by the power of God. But it was the presence of God in Moses that allowed Moses to speak out what was to happen. It was by his request to the Pharaoh that enabled the people to pack up and go.

God used Moses to show the great power of God to both the powers that be and all the slaves to be freed. He also showed those enslaved that they did not have to stay captive. God used Moses' personality and past to move things forward. The same is true for us today. God will use your personality, past, and talents to accomplish His purposes.

You might be scientifically minded, or politically minded, or technically minded, or artistic. It does not matter the direction your talents take. God has a purpose for you. Personally, I am never going to be a rocket scientist. I have met some in my life, but my brain just does not go there. I had a biology major try and help me when I was in college. It was hopeless. I still failed something that he thought was easy. His talents probably did not include singing or dancing or painting. If he became a doctor or research scientist, I am sure he did a great job at it. It just will never be me.

God has graced me with a love and grace for people. Many would call me naïve for believing people. I never start by assuming that people are going to lie to me. I believe what they say. I think it is because I believe that everyone deserves the benefit of the doubt. Innocent until proven guilty is still a truth we hold to in this country. How much easier would it be to believe it if we were more trusting in those around us? If we first believe what we are told until it is proven otherwise, we might be better off.

Do I know people lie? Yes, I do. I have been lied to, cheated on and deceived a lot in my life. Do I believe that people are basically good? Not necessarily, because I believe we have all sinned and fall short of the glory of God. However, I do believe that we need to trust one another. That has gained me trust from some people that are not too trusting. It has given me the opportunity to speak into people's lives even if they make bad choices.

It is these different personality traits that God uses to manifest His power in people's lives. In order for us to access that power, we must know what God is up to. In order to know we must focus on Him. Many scientific discoveries have been made because people focused on God and sought answers from Him instead of trial and error. I recently had someone tell me we had not cured anything in almost three quarters of a century. How many cures for diseases would we have today if only we had sought out God's answer, instead of using trial and error?

It is the power of God and listening to and obeying His direction that have saved people's lives and feed those that were hungry. Although we might not understand just how powerful something we say or do can be, it is not our purpose to show everyone how wonderful we are. And it is not for us to judge just how powerful something we say or do can be. I am sure God used Billy Graham's Sunday School teacher to help prepare him for a life of evangelism. Any idea of that name? It is not important just how important we think we can be. It is important that God knows the importance of what we do and say.

"And I will show wonders in the heaven above, And signs on the earth beneath; Blood, and fire, and vapor of smoke:" Acts 2:19

It is by God's power that great things are accomplished. We see these signs. When we look at a sunrise or sunset, we can physically see the beauty of God's creation. The heat of the sun is not what we recognize. The beauty created in the displayed colors splashed across our vision is breathtaking. Lightening or wind from a storm can destroy things that man has created. However, that same wind can be a gently blowing breeze across your face. Making it a blessing on a hot summer day.

It is important that we keep our focus on God. As that happens, we will not only see more and more signs and wonders in the world, but we will see God's purpose being fulfilled through us. A greater understanding of our purpose will be seen and accomplished. God's power will be visible.

Do Not Thank Me

Do not thank me for answering God's call
For doing what he said, for giving my all

If I was an example of Christ's Holy Love
Give thanks to the Father and look above.

Follow where you saw me to go
Seek after the Father to brighten your load

With prayer and thanksgiving and a strong dose of joy
Go where he leads you; that's my reward.

QUESTIONS TO PONDER

1. Do you see God manifested power in your life?

   _____

   _____

2. Where is your focus?

   _____

   _____

3. Do you study and research to know more on a regular basis?

   _____

   _____

4. What changes can you make to have a greater impact on others?

   _____

   _____

5. How powerful is God?

   _____

   _____

6. Do you see others and think of them as having greater power or access to God?

_____

_____

7. Do you have a story where God's manifest presence was seen?

_____

_____

8. What talent has God given to you?

_____

_____

9. How do you feel that talent can fulfill a purpose?

_____

_____

CHAPTER SEVENTEEN
THE GLORY OF THE LORD

||||||||||||||||||||||||||||||||||||||||||||||||||||||||||||||||||||||||||||||||||||||||||||||||||||||||||||||||||||||||

And the appearance of the glory of Jehovah was like devouring fire on the top of the mount in the eyes of the children of Israel. (Deut. 24:17)

Consuming fire! A consuming fire burns HOT! Can you picture a fire so hot that it is consuming the top of a mountain? What does that look like? Molten lava comes to my mind. No flame but fire so hot it has an intensity that will burn away anything that comes near. Even getting too close can cause incineration.

As I consider what happens when a fire consumes something, I imagine more of the effect than the fire itself. A consuming fire leaves nothing of the old to be salvaged. Everything is burnt, charred and left to be blown away in the wind or swept away in the cleanup. I believe God's glory is what consumes our old, sinful ways. His desire is that the sin in our lives be burned away so we can be free from its bondage. As we are born again, it is God's glory that shines through us for the world to see.

For us, this can take a moment or a lifetime. Due to the personality God has given to us, we can change in an instant or it can take years or decades to purify us. God works on each of us differently. Sanctification can depend on many things but changing us into the image of our Lord is the goal. It may be others around us that slow the cleaning we endure.

Imagine a building. It can be large or small. The roof is consumed in flames. Unquenched, the fire will spread to anything nearby. The fire is visible to everyone around. Even a small spark can cause a large blaze without being adjoined to the building. This is how God wants his glory to work in us. He wants to set us ablaze so that all can see and be affected by His glory. Just as God's glory did not consume the mountain, but appeared as a consuming fire, when we allow that glory to shine through us, the world will see.

The Scriptures show us that we are unable to withstand the glory of God. Moses asked God to see His Glory and God hid him in the cleft of a rock and covered it with His hand until He had passed by. After passing by, Moses was able to see only the Lord's glory from behind. Seeing His face would have killed Moses.

God is not out to destroy us. He wants to go with us. He wants to enjoy and be enjoyed by His creation. We do, however, have an enemy in this fallen world. The destruction and decay are because this enemy wants to destroy God's creation. Through jealously and treason, the one we know as Satan, became an enemy of God. Since his defeat and banishment, his goal has been to kill, steal and destroy, and his target is God. He works on mankind to accomplish his goal. Far too often as we look around and see the horrible things that happen in this world, we ask God why He did that to us, forgetting that it is His enemy who is out to wreak as much havoc as possible. We are in the midst of a spiritual war.

Having been born into a fallen world, we are unable to understand, without God's direction, the intensive passion and subtle nuances of Satan's war games. He is a crafty devil with thousands of years of experience. He has a lot of confidence in his methods. It takes a heart open to God's presence and direction to not be continually deceived. It takes wisdom of the Scriptures to recognize Satan's deception and lies. Each time we defeat the devil's plans, we reflect God's glory in this world.

So, when we allow God to burn up the sinful ways within us, we begin to reflect God's glory. When we study His word and learn our position over the enemy, we reflect God's glory. When we trust the Lord in our circumstances, we reflect God's glory. When we become passionate about God, we begin to be like that building – seen by all, affecting everything around us and sparking God's glory in others.

I must admit this is the hardest chapter to write. How do you explain God's glory? His glory is an invisible sight, seen only with the heart. It is displayed in the sunrise and sunset of each day but cannot be captured in a photograph or painting. It is deeply felt but is not an emotion. It is understood but cannot be explained with mere words.

In order to get a better grasp on exactly what glory is or does, I looked through the Scriptures, and rarely is it expressed in the same way. It can be seen, sung, given, declared, ascribed, revered, entered, terrifying, revealing and grow. Glory can fly, settle, appear, consecrate, fill, move, paralyze, hover, rumble and radiate. It can be expressed and celebrated. It can be prevented, faded or taken away. God **is** glory to others, and He does not yield His glory.

So how do you describe this most fascinating and unusual thing called glory? I do not think you can. The nature of glory is too diverse and complex. You know it when you see it, but expressing it eludes us. This powerful entity has no physical aspect, but we can feel it in and around us. It is a trait that you can give to others without having it yourself. You cannot even get it for yourself although there are those who seek it.

Considering how God hid Moses in the cleft of a rock so that he would not die, I believe we only see a reflection of God's glory. When we experience the greatest amount of awe from recognizing the glory of God, it is but a taste. God's desire for a relationship with us is expressed in His glory. Just as He granted Moses' request, He allows us without even asking to glimpse His glory today.

I love that glory can be celebrated. I believe that it is when we turn our hearts to celebrating God's glory that we give our most adoring praise because it is through the recognition and acknowledgement of that glory that we express our most sincere faith. Again, Hebrews 11:1 tells us, **"Now faith is [a]assurance of *things* hoped for, a [b]conviction of things not seen."** God's glory is the proof that we can trust in God and that we are placing our faith in a substantial hope. As we celebrate, our faith increases, and we are drawn closer to our Creator who desires a relationship with us.

It does not matter that God's glory cannot be defined. Simply by the fact that it is unable to be defined, we can understand the complexity of God. Although we often try to put Him in a box or define exactly who or what God is, we are always reminded that as mere mortals, it is impossible for us to capture the infinite glory of the Lord. Yet He uses that same glory through us to reflect Himself to the world. A world He loves and desires for His passion to burn within our hearts.

Painted by God's Hand

I watch a sunset and I see the glory of God

A feeling of awe arisen within me

The beauty is breathtaking

Words are not enough to express the beauty or feeling
that fills me

And in the morning, the wonder of a new day rises with
the sun

The hues painted across the sky tell of the hope for
the day

It is glorious!

It is a sight painted by the hand of God.

QUESTIONS TO PONDER

1. Give an example of God's glory in your life.

   _____

   _____

2. Where have you seen God's glory?

   _____

   _____

3. When have you felt His glory?

   _____

   _____

4. How have you seen God's glory reflected in others?

   _____

   _____

5. Like Moses, do you seek to see or know God's glory?

   _____

   _____

CHAPTER EIGHTEEN
CONSECRATION

|||||||||||||||||||||||||||||||||||||||||||||||||||||||||||||||||||||||||||||||||||||||||||||||||||||||||||||

"*[10] And Jehovah said unto Moses, Go unto the people, and sanctify them to-day and tomorrow, and let them wash their garments, [11] and be ready against the third day; for the third day Jehovah will come down in the sight of all the people upon mount Sinai. [12] And thou shalt set bounds unto the people round about, saying, Take heed to yourselves, that ye go not up into the mount, or touch the border of it: whosoever toucheth the mount shall be surely put to death: [13] no hand shall touch [a] him, but he shall surely be stoned, or shot through; whether it be beast or man, he shall not live: when the [b] trumpet soundeth long, they shall come up to the mount. [14] And Moses went down from the mount unto the people, and sanctified the people; and they washed their garments. [15] And he said unto the people, Be ready against the third day: come not near a woman.*

[16] And it came to pass on the third day, when it was morning, that there were thunders and lightnings, and a thick cloud upon the mount, and the voice of a trumpet exceeding loud; and all the people that were in the camp trembled. [17] And Moses brought forth the people out of the camp to meet God; and they stood at the nether part of the mount. [18] And mount Sinai, the whole of it, smoked, because Jehovah descended upon it in fire; and the smoke thereof ascended as the smoke of a furnace, and the whole mount quaked greatly. [19] And when the voice of the trumpet waxed

louder and louder, Moses spake, and God answered him by a voice. ²⁰ And Jehovah came down upon mount Sinai, to the top of the mount: and Jehovah called Moses to the top of the mount; and Moses went up. ²¹ And Jehovah said unto Moses, Go down, charge the people, lest they break through unto Jehovah to gaze, and many of them perish. ²² And let the priests also, that come near to Jehovah, sanctify themselves, lest Jehovah break forth upon them. ²³ And Moses said unto Jehovah, The people cannot come up to mount Sinai: for thou didst charge us, saying, Set bounds about the mount, and sanctify it." Exodus 19:10-23

What is consecration? *Webster's Dictionary* defines it as "to set apart for sacred use." In this chapter of Exodus, we see the consecration of God's people. God cannot be in the presence of sin. Therefore, the need for each coming near to be consecrated. Just after having led them out of Egypt, God camped them at the foot of Mount Sinai and set them apart as a people for Himself. He says that although the whole earth is His, these people are a treasured possession. You may be a diamond, but this nation is God's pearl. The apple of His eye. His plan is for this to be a holy nation. People set aside for His purposes. God not only has chosen a people for Himself, He has also shown us a picture of the church.

The nation of Israel are the descendants of Abraham, Isaac and Jacob. However, I do not believe these people God set aside were an exclusive group. I believe there were more people delivered from Egypt than just the descendants of Abraham. When you move more than a million people, I suspect a few aliens to be in the bunch. And so, it is with the church. God has not chosen only the Joneses or the Martinez's or the Flynts' to be set aside for sacred use. He wants all of his children to be consecrated.

Consecration is a preparation, and it is also dependent upon our actions. God did not tell Moses that He consecrated this people. He gave Moses specifics for their consecration. Specifics that we need to heed in our own lives today. God sought their obedience. He seeks our obedience today.

This preparation was not immediate. It took place over time. It would be well for us to remember that. In our instant-communication, 30-minute-solution society, we want everything now. But God does not work on our timetable. We must not assume that our desires and wishes are to be met by God when we want. Instead, we are to meet God's desires and wishes as He wants, in and for and through our lives. Our purpose on this earth is not for our own pleasure, but for His.

SHOWING OBEDIENCE AND RESTRAINT

The first thing the people were required to do for consecration was to wash their clothes. I believe this is a reflection of how the world sees us. As people set aside for sacred use, it is important that both our inward and outward actions coincide. Otherwise, the world sees hypocrisy. Just as God took the people out of Egypt, Jesus takes us and removes us from sin. It is then our responsibility to follow His commands and clean up our act as He is cleaning up our hearts. If we continue in sin, ignoring His work in our life, He will allow us to walk away. But it is important to remember that there are grave consequences in such disobedience, consequences He will allow us to face.

We see that it is not only the outward cleansing that is important, but also self-restraint. Here the people were told not to go up on the mountain. They were also told to refrain from sexual relations during this time. Self-restraint is vital when we are consecrated because we are held to a higher standard. Not only does God hold us to a higher standard, but the world expects more from God's people. Therefore, we must strive for greatness and meet the restraints that are necessary in our lives for doing God's will.

The people at the foot of Mount Sinai had to meet the restraints laid out by God. They would be stoned or shot with arrows if they went up the mountain or even touched the base. A similar parallel can be seen in today's culture. If someone steps out of line, the world is quick to throw stones. How many good people have we seen destroyed by momentary indiscretions? How many ministries have we seen die because of disobedience to God? Even through social media, we see how quickly others are willing to attack our views and opinions when they do not follow what the world considers acceptable. People are quick to take a video and post it. However, we do not get all the facts simply through that one video. Things can happen before or after that are never disclosed. It can be too late, because a myriad of people have already made up their mind as to what happened. A picture can be worth a thousand words. However, we need to listen to those thousand words to find out exactly what is meant by the picture. We do not always see clearly when given only a portion of the story.

The next step in consecration is the wait. How difficult! I think waiting on the Lord is probably the most difficult, especially when we know He has something ahead for us. We become anxious to see it fulfilled. Faith is strong in the immediate, but when we are required to wait, that same faith tends to diminish. We tend to question what we know. "Did I hear God correctly?" "Did I understand what He said?" "Did I miss something?" "Am I supposed to be doing something to make this happen?" "Did I even hear God?" We don't like to wait any more than we like to change. But it is important that our resolve today is just as strong tomorrow. Do not focus on the "I" in question. Keep your focus on God.

OUR TIME TO SEE THE LORD

When God finally descended upon the mountain to consecrate His people, it was powerful: thunder; lightening; a thick, dark cloud; a loud trumpet blast and the ground shook. This sounds more like a storm than the presence of God. But it was His presence manifesting in great power. As a matter of fact, God's presence was so real that they all trembled. I do not think this is what they were expecting. God can tell us what will happen, but we rarely expect the outcome. Our expectations are different. We forget that God's thinking is far greater than ours and the manifestations very different from our expectations.

It is important to remember that God sent a warning through Moses so that many would not perish in trying to press their way in to see the Lord. His people had to be excited to see what was going to manifest. You know, there is always one in every crowd: someone who just has to see or cannot wait his turn. Then his actions start a myriad of others to follow suit, and someone gets hurt in the process. I am sure this scene before God was no different. The Scripture does not say God gave the warning so "none" would perish. It was so "many" did not perish. God understands our impatience but warns us against rash behavior. People can get trampled in the process of our enthusiasm, and that is not God's will. It is rude and offensive when someone pushes his way ahead.

When it is our time to see the Lord, we will. When it is our time to receive His consecration, we will. Being set aside for the Lord is different for all of us. We each have our own talents, abilities and timetable for God to work in and through our lives. For some, that waiting can seem like an eternity, while others seem continually to be doing God's work with immediate results. But for some of us, there may be a longer preparation time.

GOD-GIVEN TALENT

As I think about the work that God has for each of us, I am always reminded of Proverbs 22:6, which states that you should *"Train up a child [a] in the way he should go, And even when he is old he will not depart from it."* My first thoughts, of course, are that children should be taught about the Lord and told stories from the Bible on how to praise and trust God. But it is equally as important to understand children's talents and abilities and help them develop those talents. It is also a matter of practical instruction that our children become knowledgeable about finances, work ethics, manners and respect for others. If we lack common sense, then we can be taken advantage of in life. If we struggle with our God-given talents and have not been encouraged to learn more about them, we can struggle in unrewarding jobs to simply sustain ourselves. A lack of respect, work ethics or knowledge in taking care of our finances can stifle our life and keep us from positions we need to perform as God desires.

There may be a time in your life when you will endure the frustration of just making a living and not being rewarded for your talents. Many great painters and writers such as Vincent van Gogh and Edgar Allen Poe never made money with their craft while they were alive. But since their deaths, many generations have enjoyed the rewards of their creativity. It may be true with you, too. If God consecrates, or sets you apart, for a specific purpose, you may never see any monetary gain. But God does not consecrate us for monetary gain. He consecrates us to be used to enhance life.

Everyone is talented in a different area, but all are necessary and important. Personally, I value my mechanic a great deal and could not do without my handyman. I am also enriched by my sons, whose talents are in art and computers. My neighbors are generous with their time in service for others. Never devalue your importance. Whatever your talent, God will use it to bless someone. Be prepared so that when God manifests in your life you will be like that furnace and others will see God through you.

Remember the last of this passage says that the priests must consecrate themselves or the Lord will break out against them. Even if your talents are not encouraged when you are young, you still have a responsibility to develop them when you are old enough to do so on your own. Parents do not always understand or appreciate the talents of their children. Pursue your talents and abilities so that you can always give your best for the Lord. Your parents are not accountable for what you do not pursue.

Keep your heart and mind in a position to praise, honor and trust the Lord. And do not forget that when the people consecrated themselves, there was first a physical action. What do you have in your life on a physical level that you need to clean up? That might be a continuing process. Some days are rougher than other days and require repeated efforts. Don't give up. Continually seek God's help.

Be sure you prepare for God's coming. Be watchful and wait patiently. Even when the storm hits and you are afraid, do not try to get ahead of everyone or feel you have to be there first. You do not want to trample on others. Their work and talents are also important. And most of all, remember that those who tend to just live their lives and never have a specific "calling" are sometimes the ones who are most important. It is their work that blesses others and their words of encouragement that will bolster that exceptional person. Billy Graham's Sunday school teacher played an important part in the lives of many around our world today. It was her encouragement and teaching that spurred Billy Graham to become the man he was. I am sure her legacy is rarely thought about, much less acknowledged.

Consecrate yourself and be ready for what God is going to do through your life. Continue in what you know is necessary. If a pianist played a piece two years ago and never touched that piano again, he would not be prepared to do his best in the future. You, too, need to keep alert and be prepared in every aspect so that you can perform when God calls you to your turn. Maybe you are that one that looks or feels "unimportant."

Heights Unknown

You take me to places I cannot see
My spirit to heights unknown
And all the time you dwell with me
Within I am at home

Open the eyes of my spirit
Open them so I can see
The ways and the roads ahead
Places where I need to be

Let me soar upon high like an eagle.
Let me lay in the peace of the day
Come Holy Spirit and fill me
So I can walk with you each step of the way

My road may not be so easy
My life, like roses instead
It may appear a beautiful garden
But there are thorns a plenty within

So, take me to places I cannot see
My spirit to heights unknown
And I'll dwell in your house forever
In a mansion not far from your throne

Questions to Ponder

1. "Cleanliness is next to Godliness" is a phrase we have heard throughout our lives. Do you have times that this seems a reality for you?

_____

_____

2. Do you feel like there is an inner cleansing that you need to prepare for?

_____

_____

3. Have you ever tried to "help" God?

_____

_____

4. What seems to be a long wait for you?

_____

_____

5. Have you ever been surprised by a short wait?

_____

_____

6. Are your standards for living as high was those the world imposes for you?

_____

_____

7. Which is more realistic-your standards or the worlds?

_____

_____

8. What is your biggest obstacle to self-restraint?

_____

_____

9. What are your talents and responsibilities?

_____

_____

10. Is there a difference in your feeling important and being important?

_____

_____

CHAPTER NINETEEN
TRIALS AND STRUGGLE

"⁸ Wherefore at that time certain Chaldeans came near, and brought accusation against the Jews. ⁹ They answered and said to Nebuchadnezzar the king, O king, live forever. ¹⁰ Thou, O king, hast made a decree, that every man that shall hear the sound of the cornet, flute, harp, sackbut, psaltery, and dulcimer, and all kinds of music, shall fall down and worship the golden image; ¹¹ and whoso falleth not down and worshippeth, shall be cast into the midst of a burning fiery furnace. ¹² There are certain Jews whom thou hast appointed over the affairs of the province of Babylon: Shadrach, Meshach, and Abednego; these men, O king, have not regarded thee: they serve not thy gods, nor worship the golden image which thou hast set up.

¹³ Then Nebuchadnezzar in his rage and fury commanded to bring Shadrach, Meshach, and Abednego. Then they brought these men before the king. ¹⁴ Nebuchadnezzar answered and said unto them, Is it of purpose, O Shadrach, Meshach, and Abednego, that ye serve not my god, nor worship the golden image which I have set up? ¹⁵ Now if ye be ready that at what time ye hear the sound of the cornet, flute, harp, sackbut, psaltery, and dulcimer, and all kinds of music, ye fall down and worship the image which I have made, well: but if ye worship not, ye shall be cast the same hour into the midst of a burning fiery furnace; and who is that god that shall deliver you out of my hands? [16] *Shadrach, Meshach, and Abednego answered and said to the king, O Nebuchadnezzar,* [a]*we have no need to answer thee in this matter.* [17] [b]*If it be so, our God whom we serve is able to deliver us from the burning fiery furnace; and he will deliver us out of thy hand, O king.* [18] *But if not, be it known unto thee, O king, that we will not serve thy gods, nor worship the golden image which thou hast set up."* Daniel 3:8-18

I read this and thought "WOW! What great faith!" But this passage is about the trials and struggles we encounter. These three young men were faced with a major trial. They had to decide to be obedient to God or to the king, Nebuchadnezzar. For them to be willing to lay down their life, their faith had to have grown to a point where they were a reflection of God. Such faith is the reason He was seen with them in the furnace.

Even today in cultures around the world, when people come to know Christ, they are asked when baptized if they are willing to face death. Death is a reality for many around the world because of their acceptance of Christ. Americans are blessed to not be faced with such a decision today. However, it is a reality for many throughout the world and could be a reality for us.

In Kay Arthur's Book *Lord Only You Can Change Me* there is an excellent illustration of how God uses trials and tests for our purification.

> "Do you know what I mean when I speak of 'God's crucible of purification?'" It's a word picture drawn from the ancient art of the mining and purification of silver. When silver is first extracted from the earth, it is tainted by various impurities. Purification occurs in a crucible over a hot flame. The process of heating the metal to a molten state and skimming off the impurities may be repeated as often as seven times, with each purifying fire more intense than the last. In this way, the metal

finally yields the last of its impurities, leaving pure silver behind.

During the purification process, the silversmith skims off the dross that floats to the top of the liquid silver. Looking unto the smooth pool of molten metal, the craftsman searches for his own reflected image on the surface. At first the image is very dim, and he knows that impurities remain. So, he builds the fire to an even greater intensity. He never leaves the crucible un-attended but hovers beside it, watching it closely. He repeats the process over and over until; finally, he can see a clear and perfect image of himself. When the silver becomes a mirror, he knows it is pure.

This, Beloved, is how suffering and persecution prepare us for glory. It is a fire God uses to consume the dross of our lives so that we finally reflect a clear and perfect image of Him."

This picture of the silversmith is a great explanation of the scripture in Zechariah 13:9 which states *"And I will bring the third part into the fire, and will refine them as silver is refined, and will try them as gold is tried. They shall call on my name, and I will hear them: I will say, It is my people; and they shall say, Jehovah is my God."*

In another statement, also from her book, *"Whenever expectation and reality are drastically different, trouble is on the way"*, I realized that I needed to be in the fire; the refining fire! It was that statement that helped me realize that my own expectations were seldom the reality that happens and only by allowing God to hover over me and refine me to reflect His image would my expectations draw closer to reality.

The reality of the difference in our belief, and in circumstances, can manifest in a multitude of ways. Conflict can grow greater out of differences. How drastic is this reality for you? Think about the relation-ship of two people. Although little differences can seem inconsequential when you first meet someone, they can become a major irritant as the relationship grows. The one example that comes to mind is what everyone contemplates-how spouses squeeze a tube of toothpaste. One will methodically move the toothpaste from the bottom of the tube as it empties. The other just picks it up and squeezes it in the middle. When you have a husband and wife with these two different beliefs, trouble can loom ahead. This seems like a small issue, so why is this reality so drastic? Over time, the difference becomes not about how the toothpaste is squeezed, but about what you believe about how it should be dispensed. It is because the spiritual reality or belief in our lives is much greater than we usually want to acknowledge. Whether you believe your way is the only way or whether you esteem others better than yourself reflects in how you operate. That is how a spiritual reality can cause a chasm in the physical reality. Demanding others conform to "the right way" will cause conflict, while accepting there is a difference can dispel conflict.

It is important that we move from operating at a spiritually immature level to reflecting Christ's image. Even couples who are deeply committed to Christ have troubles. It is harder when a couple is growing in different directions. None of us are immune from the trouble that two people will have in trying to live together. You must move in the same direction to grow closer. If you move in different directions, you will grow further apart. Your belief system must grow in the same direction. However, if you continue to believe that you are RIGHT and that no one is going to change you, your focus is not on God, but on yourself. You cannot reflect God's love through selfishness.

There is a great dynamic to two becoming one. This happens mentally, physically and spiritually in a marriage. When one or all of these forces pull against the other, the tear is on the heart. When two people begin to date, they first begin knowing each other mentally. They talk and learn about the things they have in common. You may not always learn the differences you have with someone right away. We often hide those differences because we want to please the person we are dating. I think this is why people always say, "Marriage is a real eye opener."

This mental melding of the minds is our first connection as husband

and wife. Or at least it should be. Our society has condoned sex before marriage, and many men and women today know each other physically before they have any real knowledge of the other person. The change in the concept of "dating" has not been a positive one. Dating should still have the concept of getting to know someone before becoming physically involved. It does not work the other way around and can be very hurtful to any future relationship.

During this mental exploration of one another, it is important to search the spiritual side as well. I believe the spiritual exploration of a partner is probably the most essential and should be one of the first things two people seek to know about one another. Often, it is the last thing that is considered, especially among immature Christians. It is so important to know what your partner thinks about Christ, the Scriptures and living life through the word. Even two Christians can have very different views about how to live in Christ. Those differences are how denominations came into being. If a couple discovers minor differences in their spirituality, they can find truth by studying together. However, if there are major differences in theology, my opinion is that you best look elsewhere for a lifetime partner. Just like the toothpaste squeeze, this is something that can become a major rift.

You should always keep in mind that you are not going to change someone to fit into a mold you sculpt. God is the potter and the only one who can change someone. If you do not like a person the way he is now, you are not going to like him when he does not fit into your mold. Find the person God has made to fit your mold or break the mold.

Once you have chosen someone for a lifetime, it is also important to continue to communicate your ideas and theology to one another. You need to make a daily effort to know your partner's thoughts and let them know yours, always keeping in mind that you both failed your last mindreading course. Otherwise, you will grow in different directions, with erroneous concepts of perceptions. You change daily and those changes need to be communicated with your partner. Recently I heard a couple say that they ask each other daily "What have you heard today that I don't know". I think that is an excellent way to communicate. Not only do you capture the others thoughts, but you can explore how each of you believes in what they say.

Remember, too, that feelings are a powerful force in our lives. They are not right or wrong, and we all need someone safe to share them with. That should be your partner. Make sure you provide a safe environment for your partner to share their feelings. Do not invalidate your partner because you either disagree or encourage them in their beliefs. Work together to bring about a resolution to any situation.

As for those who are in circumstances that have grown in different directions, remember to trust Christ to draw your paths to Him. That may require getting on a new path yourself. I have learned that the more I pray for God's help, the more He changes me. That can seem to cause greater gaps, but God knows what He is doing. He wrote the book, and we are only an ant on one of its pages. We cannot read what is there, we can only see the black ink and white page. Allow God to search for His reflection in your life and keep in mind that it takes a very hot fire for refinement.

The refiner's dross is a great picture of sin. He brings it to the surface and removes it. So does Christ. Sin does not make me who I am. Christ makes me who I am. In Him, I am none of the titles that others or even I place on myself because I am covered by the forgiveness Jesus bought for me through His death. I am being refined to His image. Therefore, I need to live according to God's word and not what the past wants or the desires of my flesh.

I must then do as the Scriptures tell me in Ephesians 6 to know how to live my life.

> *"13 Wherefore take up the whole armor of God, that ye may be able to withstand in the evil day, and, having done all, to stand. 14 Stand therefore, having girded your loins with truth, and having put on the breastplate of righteousness, 15 and having shod your feet with the preparation of the [a]gospel of peace; 16 withal taking up the shield of faith, wherewith*

ye shall be able to quench all the fiery darts of the
evil one. [17] *And take the helmet of salvation, and the*
sword of the Spirit, which is the word of God:

I must put on the full armor of God – first the belt of truth. Sometimes, we have to synch things down to hold fast to truth. Lies creep into our lives as ways to "not hurt someone's feelings" or to protect us from someone's wrath. It can be easy to believe these lies. That is why it is important to openly share things with your partner. They can see things you cannot.

The next piece of armor is the breastplate of righteousness. Using righteousness as a breastplate will guard our heart from the evils that temp us throughout our lives. People and things will distract us. Keeping a focus on righteousness will keep our hearts away from illegitimate desires. If I focus on loving others, then I am not harboring anger or heading out to murder someone. If I focus on being healthy, I am not likely to be a drug addict. But even if I fall into circumstances that are not good for me, I can focus on Christ who will bring me through those circumstances.

Then, wherever we go, it is important to remember the gospel of peace because it is Christ's light and life that we reflect. It is His good news that we must share with the rest of the world and they do not hear it through anger or discord. Sometimes, they do not hear it at all, they only see how we live our life. It is our example that speaks the good news of Jesus. Be sure to speak God and his word to those around you, even if you never say anything.

Life bombards us on a daily basis. Whether we stand or fall depends on us holding tightly to our faith to shield us from the lies, temptations and hurts. It is vital to use faith as a shield to keep away what society tells us is right but what we know to be wrong. Peer pressure does not go away once you leave school. It exists in our schools, our workplaces, our churches and our homes. You must hold tight to Jesus Christ if you want to survive. As we remind ourselves of Christ's faithfulness and the benefits we receive from His sacrifice, we will cherish our salvation.

Finally, with all of these things, is the sword of the Spirit. If we are to have confidence to walk in strength and wisdom, we must have the Holy Spirit. A sword is not only a defensive weapon. Sometimes it is necessary as an offensive weapon. We must not only defend ourselves from evil attacks but cut off things in our life that hinder our growth and relationship with Christ. Anything we allow between ourselves, and Christ must be cut off.

Every step we take in our beliefs, whether it is putting on the full armor of God, prayer, study of the scriptures, or obedience to righteousness, grows our walk of faith that we can withstand the trials and struggles life throws at us.

When you stand firm in your faith, you may offend others. The declarations of "tolerance" that we hear so much of today is not a Christian principle. To live as Christ did, we cannot tolerate sin. It is not possible to be politically correct and a strong example of Christ today. That is a line you will have to choose which side to stand on. Although it may seem that one political party is closer to the truth than the other, remember that each has its own hazards. Just as each denomination has rules and expectations, so do political parties. If you choose Christ, it will not be popular. The Scriptures tell us in Matthew 7:13-14:

> "*13 Enter ye in by the narrow gate: for wide [a] is the gate, and broad is the way, that leadeth to destruction, and many are they that enter in thereby. 14 [b] For narrow is the gate, and straitened the way, that leadeth unto life, and few are they that find it.*"

Seek life! Accept the struggles because you will have them whatever road you take. The rewards for following Christ Jesus are great.

A Time Of New Beginnings

It's a time of new beginnings
To let old things pass away
Time for moving forward
Leaving things of yesterday

Going beyond the ordinary
Stepping out and stepping up
Searching new tomorrows
Learning more to trust

There's a road that lies before me
An unfamiliar journey ahead
Life's continuing adventure
Holds excitement and a little dread

The lessons from past journeys
Each one a flickering flame
It's light, an illumination
For the steps I've yet to take

A future full of endeavors
Worshiping God and following him
Searching for unknown answers
Walking in faith, and praying about what's ahead

Going where he needs me to go
Staying close by his side
Watching for his footprints
Keeping with his stride

It's a time of new beginnings
A fresh future lies ahead
Rejoice with me for fulfillment
Of Christ's love through me performed

QUESTIONS TO PONDER

1. What is your greatest trial?

_____

_____

2. What is your biggest struggle?

_____

_____

3. How do you need to strengthen your faith?

_____

_____

4. Who or what stands in your way of trusting God?

_____

_____

5. How drastic is the difference between your circumstances and your faith?

_____

_____

6. Without looking in Ephesians six, can you name the armor of God you need to put on each day?

_____

_____

7. If you failed to remember them all, what piece of armor do you fail to put on each day?

_____

_____

8. Are you willing to sacrifice people's opinions for your faith?

_____

_____

9. Are you willing to sacrifice your life for your faith?

_____

_____

Conclusion

It begins with a spark, a flicker of heat searching for fuel. A flame will begin to burn when it is sufficiently fanned and provided with fuel. So must our spirit be fueled by God and fanned by our willingness to allow the flame of the Holy Spirit to burn in our lives.

In the hands of wisdom, a fire is beautiful and can provide warmth. But once it rages out of control, you can be burned, and destruction is assured.

> *"[11] And I saw a great white throne, and him that sat upon it, from whose face the earth and the heaven fled away; and there was found no place for them. [12] And I saw the dead, the great and the small, standing before the throne; and books were opened: and another book was opened, which is the book of life: and the dead were judged out of the things which were written in the books, according to their works. [13] And the sea gave up the dead that were in it; and death and Hades gave up the dead that were in them: and they were judged every man according to their works. [14] And death and Hades were cast into the lake of fire. This is the second death, even the lake of fire. [15] And if any was not found written in the book of life, he was cast into the lake of fire."*
> *(Revelation 20:11-15)*

Living in the spiritual fire embraces the covenant God made with us and deepens our commitment to stand on faith through trials and testing. It allows us to be consecrated for God's glory and for His purposes. In doing so, we are blessed with an abundant and fulfilling life; not one that is untouched by trials, but a life that develops through the word and worship and grows in wisdom and faith because of the continuous presence of God.

"Through our great good fortune, in our youth our hearts were touched with fire. It was given to us to learn at the outset that life is a profound and passionate thing." Oliver Wendell Holmes (1841-1935)

I pray that in your youth you found the Lord and that you trust Him throughout your life. If you have not yet discovered the love that burns for you, ask the Lord for His guidance and surrender your heart for His Holy Spirit to fill.

Life is profound and should be lived with passion, but passion needs fuel. There must be a source to keep the flame of passion burning or else we burn out. God is that source. Even when life begins to leave us nothing but ashes, God will use His word to rekindle the spark that seems to have gone out.

As we grow older, our passions change – sometimes from necessity. You do not find 50-year-old football stars in the thick of the game. But the passion of our youth can change and be given to others. Instead of being in the game, the 50-year-old football star may coach or referee. Maybe he is a mentor to a youth league. Our passions may take different paths a number of times in our lives, but nothing is diminished; the flames have simply changed course. The same is true with faith. The one flame we must always be careful to fan is the desire for the Lord. The faith we found in our youth will change and grow. We must not allow disappointment or discouragement to sway our beliefs. Remember, there are trials. I once heard someone say, "We all have a testimony, but the first part is the test." I also heard someone add that the teacher is always silent during the test. What a great analogy of how God works in our lives. He does test us, but only to demonstrate what we are capable of accomplishing. I believe God has much more faith in us than we do in ourselves.

I pray for God to control the fire in my life and yours. May the refining fire purify and the zealous flame of passion for the gospel burn brightly as a light for the world.

"that the proof of your faith, being more precious than gold that perisheth though it is proved by fire, may be found unto praise and glory and honor at the revelation of Jesus Christ" 1 Peter 1:7

QUESTIONS TO PONDER

1. Do you know Jesus Christ as your personal savior?

    _____

    _____

2. What steps do you feel you need to take to grow in Christ?

    _____

    _____

3. Can you face test, trials and temptations more easily knowing they are coming?

    _____

    _____

4. Do you recognize God's presence or glory around you?

    _____

    _____

5. Once you have walked through God's fire, do you experience it again?

    _____

    _____

6. Did you find these chapters to be of any benefit in your life?

_____

_____

ENDNOTES

|||||||||||||||||||||||||||||||||||||||||||||||||||||||||||||||||||||||||||||||||||||||||||||||||||||||||||||||||||||||||||||||||||||||||||

1. Ephesians 6:10
2. How Stuff Works, A Discovery Company by Tom Harris. http://science.howstuffworks.com/environmental/earth/geophysics/fire.htm
3. Ecclesiastes 1:9
4. Isaiah 55:11
5. God later changed Abram's name to Abraham. You will see him referred to both ways throughout this book.
6. Vine, W. E., Vine's Expository Dictionary of Old and New Testament Words, (Grand Rapids, MI: Fleming H. Revell) 1981.
7. John 10:10
8. American Standard Version (ASV) Public Domain

FURTHER READING

||||||||||||||||||||||||||||||||||||||||||||||||||||||||||||||||||||||||||||||||||||||||||||||||||||||||||||||||||||||

Pamela Flynt Knight also has published several other books including:

Sufficient Grace, (poetry)

Legendary Locals of Grand Prairie (a history)

Rude Awakening or Not in the Budget (real estate)

Buy, Rent, Sell - 100+ Things That Can Go Wrong (real estate)

Why Are You Here? (profiles of some local Pregnancy Resource Center volunteers, employees and steering committee members).

The limited edition poetry coffee table book, *Sufficient Grace* and the first edition of *Living in the Fire* are only available through contact with Pamela via email at pffaye@yahoo.com.

---

i.   How Stuff Works, a Discovery Company by Tom Harris http://science.howstuffworks.com/environmental/earth/geophysics/fire.html
ii. James 1:13 God does not tempt us.

Printed in the United States
by Baker & Taylor Publisher Services